**To my mother**

## Early Praise for Know Your Angels

■ Readers of books about angels will already know John Ronner as the author of *Do You Have a Guardian Angel?*, one of the earliest recent angel books. In fact, this perennial favorite has been around for nearly a decade, and still sells steadily. Readers will undoubtedly put John's new book in the same category... The stories that John has found are fascinating... Know Your Angels is truly a fun book.
**Eileen Freeman, editor of AngelWatch Journal and author of Touched by Angels**

■ A mini-encyclopedia of famous angels.
**The Grand Rapids Press**

■ (Ronner) felt that the market needed an objective, eclectic, popularly written, cross-cultural approach. His *Know Your Angels: The Angel Almanac with Biographies of 100 Prominent Angels in Legend and Folklore -- And Much More!* is just that.
**Publishers Weekly**

■ Fun to read!
**Terry Lynn Taylor, author of Messengers of Light and Guardians of Hope**

**An angel appears to the ancient Israelite leader Joshua (Gustave Dore illustration)**

# know your angels

## The Angel Almanac with Biographies of 100 Prominent Angels in Legend & Folklore – and Much More!

Published by:

**Mamre Press**
**107 South Second Avenue**
**Murfreesboro TN 37130**

Cover by Sheila Bartlett

**Library of Congress Cataloging-in-Publication Data**
Ronner, John, 1951-
    Know Your Angels: the Angel Almanac with Biographies
    of 100 Prominent Angels in Legend and Folklore, and
    Much More / John E. Ronner
          p. cm.
    Includes index.
    ISBN 0-932945-40-6 (pbk.): $10.95
1. Angels. 2. Angels -- Folklore. I. Title.
BL477.R664  1993
291.2'15 -- dc20        93-20336

Manufactured in the United States of America

## A Note From the Author

I can still remember how jolting and heartwarming it felt the first time I seriously entertained the idea that a spiritual world *just might actually exist.* Maybe my universe wasn't really just a big, cold, dead, random machine slowly running out of gas -- lacking any purpose, making no sense, and going nowhere but to oblivion. In other words, maybe the scientific materialists -- the guys who think the physical is all there is -- were wrong, cosmically wrong. That was a pleasant, buoyant lift -- even though, at the time, I was one of those guys. I had just read Raymond Moody's *Life After Life*, his account of the near-death experience which provided, in my mind at least, very strong circumstantial evidence that there is more to this world than meets the physical eye. I began to change my mind about things. Later, I happened across a book on the subject of angels, and I was struck with this thought: If there could be a spiritual world, after all, then that means that even something as "irrelevant and silly" as angels could also exist! I felt another pleasant, buoyant lift and a real fascination for the idea that something higher than we might be looking after us. But in those olden days of the mid-1970s, it seemed the angel book usually fell into one of two categories -- a lightly researched whimsical eclectic treatment or a one-sided religious tract designed to convert the reader to this sect or that one. For seven years, I searched without satisfaction for the particular kind of book I most wanted to read -- a heavily researched, popularly written, newspaper-style treatment of the subject of angels.

Finally, in 1983, having worked as a newspaper reporter for much of my adult life, I decided to assign myself the story, so to speak. In my spare time, I spent 14 months gathering information and ended up with 110 file folders stuffed with notes. *Do You Have a Guardian Angel?* appeared in 1985 and, to my delight, immediately began selling. And I soon noticed something I had not expected: Many of those who were buying the book, it turned out, were not just looking for entertainment or buying out of idle curiosity; they themselves had had the kinds of dramatic angel encounters being described in the book.

I suppose my little story is a microcosm of our entire Western culture. Imagine: a whole civilization slowly changing its mind in the late 20th Century about the basic nature of reality. We don't really have much of a choice, what with the new findings from quantum physics strongly suggesting that our physical reality is, in a sense, indeed the illusion that mystics have always said it was; astrophysicists talking about how time and space did not yet exist in the infinitesimally small fraction of a second after the Big Bang (Can you imagine such a universe?); the Anthropic Principle, which has convinced many leading thinkers that we live in a "designer universe" against all odds. And many more new developments now fermenting. Every day, we see more and more clearly how the old worn-out world view of materialism is shot through with gaping holes. The West is like Rip Van Winkle waking up from a 400-year-old session of self-hypnosis.

In this new climate, where the universe is increasingly seen as a living entity backed by unseen intelligence and guidance, it shouldn't be any surprise that the angels are once again fledging their wings.

In this latest offering, I wanted to provide a fun-to-read but useful one-stop angel reference. This is an almanac of far-flung facts and fancies from hundreds of scattered sources all brought "under one roof." And the information is easy to get and use, thanks to an exhaustive index. This book is for the angel enthusiast, those who have simply encountered angels and have specific questions about their experiences, those who want to know what folklore and legend say about particular angels, ministers needing material, researchers, trivia buffs, and of course, the merely curious. -- John Ronner

**Abdiel**. During the War in Heaven, Abdiel was the only angel under Satan's command who refused to rebel against God. Blasphemously making himself a mountain throne in heaven, Satan first had to talk his subordinates into following his scheme for a rebellion. Speaking to an assembly of the angels under him, Satan blasted his followers for obeying God, calling their loyal service a nasty "prostration" and saying that they were really meant to rule, not to be servile underlings. Abdiel, however, heckled Satan, saying that the idea of a created being rebelling against his Maker was crazy -- like a puppet turning against the puppet-maker who held its strings. Abdiel argued that Satan had to be weaker than God since God created him. Satan shot back that, no, he was not a created being -- which was another lie from the Father of Lies. Abdiel just says no -- flying away, leaving his more impressionable colleagues behind to be manipulated and tricked into going along with Satan's cosmic error. The complete tale is told in Puritan John Milton's 12-volume epic poem *Paradise Lost*.

**Abraham's Three Angels**. In the Bible's Book of Genesis, these are the three angels on their way to destroy the sinful cities Sodom and Gomorrah. Beforehand, though, disguised as mortals, they stop at the tent of the ancient father of the Hebrew race, Abraham. The hospitable Abraham gives the secret angels water for their dusty feet, shade under a tree and a meal of calfmeat, cream and baked bread -- winning their favor unawares. Perhaps referring to this Old Testament legend, the New Testament writer of the letter to the Hebrews says: "Remember to welcome strangers in your home. There were some who did that and welcomed angels without knowing it." In our own time, there is a whole class of stories in which angels are believed to have disguised themselves as humans in order to render help under the most uncanny circumstances.

**Acts of the Holy Angels**. From time to time, artists have painted a series of 11 Biblical scenes which are called collectively the *Acts of the Holy Angels.* Usually the 11 scenes include: 1. The fall of Lucifer. 2. The banishment of Adam and Eve from the Garden of Eden. 3. The visit by the three angels to Abraham, who fails to recognize them as angels but wins their favor by showing kindness and hospitality. 4. The angel who stops Abraham from sacrificing his son Isaac at God's command. 5. The Dark Angel wrestling with the Hebrew patriarch Jacob at Peniel. 6. Angels ascending and descending "Jacob's Ladder." 7. The saving of the three children from the fiery furnace. 8. The angel slaying the army of the Assyrian Emperor Sennacherib who was laying seige to Jerusalem. 9. Raphael protecting Tobias. 10. Heliodorus' punishment. 11. Gabriel's announcement to the Virgin Mary that she would bear Jesus.

**Aeons**. As infant Christianity spread like wildfire through the Roman Empire during the 100s and 200s A.D., it had stiff competition from another big and growing religion, *gnosticism*. In gnosticism, the angels were called *aeons*. At their birth, the aeons were just abstract Godly Characteristics, like Love and Truth. But these hazy Divine Ideas gradually "solidified" into actual living beings, and then trouble began.

In one of many contradictory gnostic legends, this one cited by writer Malcolm Godwin, God's vice-regent Satan-el, who happened to be Jesus' brother, rebelled against God. Satan-el, and one third of the angels who followed him, all fell because of their evil. These bad angels fell to the lower levels of the universe, where Satan-el created the physical world -- basically evil and empty of God. In fact, the physical world was at the mercy of the evil angels who ruled it. Why? Because the world was too far away from God to be influenced by Him. (Critics have attacked the gnostics for centuries for saying that the physical world is basically evil and godless). But despite this terrible situation of an evil world, all was not lost for the mortals who were stuck there. Luckily, mortals have a "divine spark" trapped within their physical bodies. (This divine spark is a dim, sleepy awareness that mortals are really heavenly citizens who ought to be living in the high heaven with their good Creator, not on earth under the thumb of the bad aeons). As mortals get enlightened, their sleepy divine spirits "wake up" to the truth of where they belong. After death, the awakened spirit tries to escape from the prison of the evil physical world and flit upward to the far-away Supreme Being in the highest heaven and to his good aeons. The jealous evil aeons, in the lower heavens, try to block the upward movement of the mortals' divine spirits. The bad aeons' goal: to keep as many souls as possible in their power, trapped in the evil physical world. In fact, there is a cosmic World War III going on between good and bad aeons behind the scenes.

**Af**. An angel of death who once swallowed Moses up to his circumcised member, according to Jewish legend. While Moses was stuck in that position, his wife Zipporah figured out what had gone wrong: God was angry with Moses for neglecting to circumcise their first-born son Gershom. Zipporah then wisely circumcised Gershom, sprinkling the blood from the wound on Moses' feet. This softened God's wrath, and a divine voice shouted down from heaven: "Spew him out!" Af obediently vomited out Moses. Then, Moses resumed his return from exile, back to Egypt, to free the enslaved Hebrews. Details of this strange encounter may be found in volume II of Louis Ginzberg's *The Legends of the Jews* and author Gustav Davidson's *A Dictionary of Angels*.

**Ahriman**. See Angra Mainyu.

**Ahura Mazda**. ("The Wise Lord") This is the one true god in the ancient Persian religion of Zoroastrianism, once one of the world's great religions until it was virtually destroyed by the Moslem conquest of Persia in the 600s A.D. (About 250,000 Zoroastrians survive today in Iran and India). Ahura Mazda, the god of goodness, created the light that fills the universe. Indeed, the *Avesta*, the Zoroastrian bible, describes the sun and moon as his eyes. Ahura Mazda, his six helping archangels (Good Mind, Truth, Power, Devotion, Health and Life), and lower angels are continually at war with Ahura Mazda's evil twin Ahriman and his devils. At death, every mortal will be judged at the Bridge of Discrimination for assignment to heaven or hell. But fortunately, the Zoroastrian hell is not everlasting.

At the end of time, all evil will be purged from the universe, and every creature will return to goodness and truth. Many scholars believe that Zoroastrian ideas of warfare between good and evil angels caused some ancient Jews to adopt the notion of angel combat, and eventually Christianity, too, since Christianity was built upon Judaism. (See Ahriman).

**Al Arat**. This is the Moslem limbo, a haven for pre-muslim patriarchs and prophets; ordinary humans whose good and evil on earth is evenly balanced; or small children and insane people, according to some interpreters of a Koran passage describing this afterlife realm. Al Arat lacks both the joys of heaven and the agonies of hell, but its dwellers will eventually get to heaven at Doomsday.

**Amesha Spentas**. See "Holy Immortals."

**Angel**. In the strictest definition, an angel is a superior being living in the spirit world -- standing between humans and God in the cosmic order. Philosophers have argued over whether human beings slowly evolve into angels or whether angels are a separate, higher order of being and neither angel nor human can ever become the other. Regardless of the debate, in the popular mind, the terms "angel" and "guardian angel" are very loosely used. Some people's so-called "guardian angels" do indeed seem to act like superior beings (e.g. A witness might describe seeing an overwhelmingly loving and dynamic being of light, among other things). But other people's "guardian angels" seem to be what might be more strictly termed "guardian spirits" -- mortals who have died but continue to look after their loved ones from beyond the grave. This is commonly reported among widows and widowers separated by death, and also parents and children. Still others feel that the appearance of what seems to be a superior spiritual being might actually be the so-called *higher self* of the individual; in other words, the sum of his earthly incarnations, according to one viewpoint. And complicating all this even more is a class of stories in which people feel that the angel -- as a superior being -- has disguised itself as a mortal to help them. The confusion extends beyond what an angel is to what an angel does: "Angelic intervention" for one person might be the action of an outside, heavenly entity. But to another, the event might be explained as a *synchronicity* or meaningful coincidence, or perhaps the working of the subconscious mind on a psychic level.

**Angel Authors**. Of the modern angel book authors, one of the first to make a major splash was evangelist Billy Graham, whose *Angels: God's Secret Agents* appeared in the mid-1970s, provided an evangelical Protestant perspective and sold more than a million copies. One of the most successful angel authors of the early 1990s is Sophy Burnham, whose eclectic 1990 *Book of Angels* soared to more than 300,000 copies in print within just two years of publication. Burnham's book demonstrated again, like Graham's book, the sales potential for angel books, and publishers this time were noticing. As angel publishing heated up, the field developed different focuses. Some authors, like John Ronner in his 1985 *Do You Have a Guardian Angel?*, took a newspaper-style, journalistic approach.

Others, like Terry Lynn Taylor in her 1990 *Angels: Messengers of Light*, combined the angel theme with self-help advice. Some authors produced books specializing in techniques for contacting one's guardian angel, such as Jane Howard's 1992 *Commune with the Angels*. One popular new category was the angel letter book -- a collection of personal letters relating angel experiences sent to an author by readers who enjoyed the author's original angel book. Examples: Burham's *Angel Letters* (1991), and Taylor's *Answers From the Angels* (1993). On the other hand, Joan Wester Anderson's 1992 *Where Angels Walk* is a collection of gripping angel encounter narratives. Incidentally, the first angel book author in what is now the United States was the Puritan minister and Harvard University President Increase Mather, who penned *Angelographia* in 1696. Mather may have decided to write the book because of the Salem witch trials, according to Eileen Freeman, writing in the January-February 1993 issue of AngelWatch newsletter. (See AngelWatch)

**Angel Books**. See the bibliography for a comprehensive listing of angel books.

**Angel Collectors Club of America**. Founded in 1976, this growing organization's 1,000-plus members collect angel representations of every type. This includes figurines, ornaments, dolls, angels on postcards and paper angels. Beyond collecting, the members have a general interest in angelology. They share their angel knowledge in talks before church groups, at retirement homes and in other locations.

Oftentimes, these collections become the subjects of feature articles in newspapers. The ACCA's chatty quarterly newsletter is titled *Halo Everybody!* Members correspond, there are area chapter meetings regularly to talk about places of interest to angel lovers and spots where angel articles can be purchased. A national convention is scheduled biennially. For more information, contact Blanche Thompson at 533 E. Fairmont Drive, Tempe AZ 85282.

**Angel Holidays.** In the Roman Catholic Church calendar, Oct. 2 is the day for honoring guardian angels. A few days earlier, Sept. 29, is the feast day for the three angels mentioned by name in the Bible -- Michael, Gabriel and Raphael. That day was formerly in honor only of Michael, with Gabriel having a separate day on March 24 and Raphael a day on Oct. 24. When the church calendar was reformed in 1969, the three occasions were merged. In England, the old feast day for Michael alone was called *Michaelmas*, and families had a custom of eating roast goose. On July 28, Ethiopian and Egyptian Orthodox Christians celebrate an annual feast in honor of the angel Uriel (See Uriel).

**Angel Language.** In folklore, the native language of angels seems to depend on cultural point of view. Ancient and medieval rabbis were certain that the language of angels is Hebrew, which is supposedly the language not only of angels, but was the tongue of Adam and Eve and the tempting serpent at Eden and indeed God's native language when He created the world. In fact, not until God deliberately thwarted the builders of the heaven-scaling Tower of Babel by giving them different languages did Hebrew stop being humankind's universal speech -- so the thinking went. Some Catholics have believed that angel talk is in Latin, while Moslems believe that Gabriel communicated in Arabic with Mohammed. In philosophy, certain leading thinkers, like Thomas Aquinas, the Middle Ages' top angel scholar, don't champion individual earthly languages. Instead, they suggest, the actual language of angels is a wordless exchange of thoughts -- "illumination" to use Aquina's term, "telepathy," to use ours.

**Angel of Death**. In the Old Testament, this is an angel to whom God delegates the power to bring death to mortals. In Jewish lore, the angel of death is often a cruel, soul-snatching heavenly being, but he does act under God's orders. Some say the angel of death is covered with eyes so that no mortal on earth can escape his baleful attention. In many stories, the angel of death is disguised as a human wanderer, much as Bible legend's first murderer, the farmer Cain, became a homeless nomad after taking his shepherd brother Abel's life in the Book of Genesis. Many Jewish legends have the angel of death showing up to claim his doomed victim at the worst possible moment -- a newlywed couple's wedding night. Naturally, a struggle breaks out, in which the angel of death is sometimes tricked and cheated, or sometimes he takes pity and relents to come another day. To the Jews, the angel of death was often identified with the fierce angel Samael, who was once beaten and blinded by Moses (pummeled by his famous rod) for trying to bring death to the Lawgiver before he was ready. To Christians, the angel of death is Michael, and to the Moslems, Azrael.

Legend and folklore aside, in modern times, people who have nearly died often report meeting loved ones -- mortal friends and relatives who died before they did, who act as their guides in the afterlife. Or the person brushing with death may see a superior angel-like being with a body of light who displays an overwhelming love and compassion, helps them examine their lives on earth from a spiritual standpoint and ultimately sends them back to living.

**Angel of the Furnace**. During the "Babylonian Captivity" of the 500s B.C. (when Jewish leaders were being held hostage in Babylon to make sure the Jews did not revolt again against the Babylonian Empire), there were three Jewish officials, Shadrach, Meshach and Abednego, who risked their lives for their beliefs but were saved by an unnamed angel, according to a legend in the Old Testament Book of Daniel. The trouble had begun when the three refused to bow down to a new golden idol, which they considered a false god. The Babylonian King Nebuchadnezzer flew into a rage and ordered them pitched into a fiery furnace stoked seven times hotter than normal. So hot that the henchmen tossing the trio inside were themselves burned up. But soon, the king jumped to his feet, amazed: Not only were the three walking around inside unharmed, but they were joined by a fourth figure who "looks like an angel." Eventually, the three walked out of the furnace unscathed, and a chastened Nebuchadnezzer ordered that anyone who spoke disrespectfully of the Hebrew God be torn limb from limb. (The king was making an effort, at least, but any lesson of religious tolerance had obviously not yet taken hold).

**Angel of the Lord**. When the Bible's Old Testament talks about the "Angel of the Lord," it is often referring to the presence of God Himself, not necessarily to an angel in the ordinary meaning of the word.

**Angel of Peace**. The angel of peace guides the soul of a good man when he dies, according to the *Testament of Benjamin*. So it is logical that it is the angel of peace that guides the righteous Old Testament patriarch Enoch on his trip to the first heaven in the *Slavonic Book of Enoch*. (In general folklore, Enoch made this trip without having to die and was turned into the angel Metatron. See Metatron.)

**Angel Wrapped in a Cloud**. This unnamed angel appeared to John of Patmos during his vision of the end of the world, reported in the New Testament's Book of Revelation. The angel's face shone like the sun, his body was wrapped in a cloud, he had a rainbow over his head, and his legs were fiery columns, one resting on sea, one on land. The angel swore that the end of time had come. And he gave John a book to eat, which tasted like honey in his mouth, but was sour in his stomach, once swallowed.

**Angelolatry**. The veneration of angels. The whole ancient Christian Church was confused over how angels should be treated, as some leaders okayed the idea of revering the beings while others scorned it as "masked idolatry." About 300 years after Rome fell, a gathering of Christian bishops decided it was all right to deeply honor angels, but that worship should be reserved for God alone.

**Angelology**. The study of angels.

**Angelophany**. An angel visitation.

**Angelos**. This is the ancient Greek word that the modern English word "angel" comes from. To ancient Greeks, *angelos* meant just an ordinary human "messenger." So why is modern English using what was once an ancient word for humans to mean heavenly beings? And, what's more, why is a **Greek** word being used for a Judaeo-Christian idea that goes back to the **Hebrew** Old Testament? Here's what happened: The original Hebrew word in the Bible for an angelic messenger of God was *malakh*. Beginning in the 200s B.C., Jewish scholars began translating the Hebrew Old Testament into Greek for two reasons. Jews were losing the ability to read Hebrew, and Greek had become a lingua franca, an international language, for the Near East (much as English has become today's world language). The translators were looking for a good Greek word to render *malakh* into Greek. Two Greek candidates readily availed themselves: *angelos* (ordinary messenger) and *daimon* (a guardian spirit that could influence a person for good or an evil spirit that could cause harm -- Socrates, for example, said he had a good *daimon*). The translators chose the relatively neutral word *angelos* over *daimon* with its more complicated and potentially misleading meaning. Over the centuries,*daimon* changed its meaning, no longer referring to both good or bad spirits influencing people. It started meaning only an evil spirit. The word then became the basis for the modern English word *demon*.

**Dante and Beatrice reach Jupiter during their climb through the various heavens. (A Gustav Dore illustration for The Divine Comedy)**

**Angels Can Fly**. Best-selling angel book author Terry Lynn Taylor's chatty, inspirational and informative newsletter mixes articles on angel themes with lively letters from readers and resources for angel enthusiasts. Taylor's first two angel books, *Messengers of Light* and *Guardians of Hope* had a combined 140,000 copies in print within two years of publication -- popular in part because of their positive tone. For more information, write: Angels Can Fly, P.O. Box 80471, San Marino CA 91118-8471.

**Angels Disguised as Humans**. This is one of the most common categories of angel encounter, where individuals feel that an angel disguised as a human being has helped them in an uncanny way. Consider this composite encounter, blending together the elements that often crop up: A woman's car breaks down on a deserted road. She's nervous, because she hasn't seen any traffic for some time. Suddenly, a truck appears out of nowhere. A pleasant but rather quiet man emerges. He happens to have just the right tool necessary to fix the engine and knows how to use it. The stranger seems to know things about the motorist that he shouldn't, perhaps even calling her by name. Indeed, if the motorist has needed some comforting about a secret which is troubling her, the stranger uncannily zeros in on this unspoken concern and provides a reassuring word or some enlightening advice. When he is asked questions about himself, he persistently avoids giving information. The motorists' mood is lifted. Her attention is diverted momentarily as the truck drives off, and when she glances back a second or two later, the truck is nowhere to be seen on the highway, despite excellent visibility.

**Angels of Mons**. Did angels intervene on the battlefield shortly after World War I broke out? In August 1914, scores of stories began cropping up about how angels and long-dead saints were appearing along Western Europe's war front to help Allied soldiers retreating from Mons, Belgium. As a German offensive drove back desperate British and French soldiers, many of these troops began reporting visions of St. George, England's patron saint; Joan of Arc, France's patron; angelic cavalry; a golden-armored archangel Michael atop a white horse; the Virgin Mary and so on.

In one story, a group of British soldiers, trapped in a trench, charged out of their pocket against the Germans, shouting "St. George for England." As the soldiers ran, an officer with the unit became aware of a large company of men with bows and arrows going along with him and even leading him on against the enemy's trenches. And afterward, when this British officer was talking to a German prisoner, the German asked him who was the officer on a great white horse who led them? For although he was such a conspicuous figure, none of the Germans had been able to shoot him. Actually, the British officer himself did not see any mysterious "officer on the white horse" (identified as St. George); the British soldier only claimed to have seen the phantom archers that St. George supposedly was leading. (The British officer told his story to a correspondent for the Catholic publication *Universe*, and the account appeared in Harold Begbie's book *On the Side of the Angels*.)

Meanwhile, in another area of the war front, a retreating British company claimed an angel troop interposed itself between the Britons and pursuing German cavalry.

This intervention caused the German horses to rear, wheel and stampede. The British used the confusion to escape. In still another story, a war front chaplain, the Rev. Oswald Watkins, asserted that French soldiers claimed to be seeing a mysterious "nurse" tending dying soldiers at the Battle of Ypres who looked like the Virgin Mary.

On another occasion, a wounded lance corporal claimed that his soldiers watched in silent awe for a half-hour as three shining figures with faces hovered in the sky above them -- one of the celestial trio seeming to have outstretched wings. The event allegedly began just after the corporal's army battalion had beaten back a German attack. At that point, a greatly upset captain approached the corporal, asking if he or any of his soldiers had seen anything "astonishing." The captain then led the corporal and several soldiers to a treeless area to show them the unobstructed sky. "I could see quite plainly in mid-air a strange light...," the corporal said in a formal statement to nursing supervisor Courtney Wilson, reported in Begbie's book. "The light became brighter, and I could see quite distinctly three shapes." The three figures had long, loose-hanging golden-colored garments, and they hovered above the German line, facing the British soldiers, the corporal told Wilson. As the troops watched the spectacle, according to the corporal, "one of the chaps called out, 'God's with us!' and that kind of loosened us."

During the Allied retreat from Mons, soldiers who were once skeptical about the supernatural often showed a change of heart. Some of them eagerly sought out pictures of St. Michael (the archangel) and Joan of Arc, according to an article in the August 1915 issue of *Occult Review* written by volunteer war front nurse Phyllis Campbell -- an article also reported on in Begbie's book. One day, a Lancashire infantryman asked Campbell for a picture or medal of St. George, claiming that he had seen the saint on a white horse leading the British at Vitry-le-Francois. "It's true, Sister, we all saw it," another soldier reportedly told Campbell. This incident began just after a large number of German soldiers had started to charge the British line. At that point, British soldiers saw a "yellow-like mist" rising into the air. The mist then "cleared off" to reveal a tall man with yellow hair and golden armor. This entity was astride a white horse, holding up a sword to urge on the British. The Germans began falling back, and the British pursued them.

Finally, a footnote to add to all these stories: In September, 1914, after the supernatural visions surrounding the Allied retreat from Mons, things got even more complicated. Arthur Machen published a fictional short story in *The London Evening News* about shining, ghostly archers from the medieval battlefield at Agincourt (scene of a great British victory in 1415 during the Hundred Years' War between England and France.) In Machen's fictional story, these long-dead bowmen appeared on World War I's western front to cover the British retreat from Mons. Machen argued that the actual supernatural reports from the war front were just imaginary hysteria touched off by his short story. Begbie, however, countered that Machen was giving himself too much credit and offered his 1915 book as evidence of that.

**In Christian legend, Christ storms hell to liberate trapped pre-Christian heros, prophets and patriarchs. (Albrecht Duerer woodcut)**

Was it all just imagination, actual angels, ghosts of slain soldiers, or perhaps a tapping into archetypes out of the collective unconscious?

**Angels of Truth and Peace**. In Jewish lore, the angels of truth and peace got into big trouble for frankly expressing their disapproval to God of his idea to create man. In those pre-First Amendment days, these two angels, and all the choirs following them, were incinerated for their indiscreet candor.

**Angels of the World**. Founded in the mid-1980s, Angels of the World is a 200-plus member group devoted to the study and enjoyment of things angelic. Many of these angel enthusiasts are collectors of various angel-oriented items. There are local chapters around the country and a bimonthly newsletter called *Notes and Comments*. For information, write to: Angels of the World, 1334 South Reisner, Indianapolis IN 46221.

**AngelWatch newsletter**. A periodical giving hard news and feature stories on angels. This bimonthly newsletter reads like a daily newspaper and has a professional look. In each issue, editor Eileen Freeman, who holds a doctorate in theology from Notre Dame, also provides a resource section listing angel clubs, angel-oriented religious groups, mail order/retail stores and publications. Beyond the journalism, Freeman has reported her own encounter with a guardian angel, a figure bathed in light who, she says, appeared to her one night when she was a small child frightened after the death of a grandmother. "Do not be afraid, Eileen. Your grandmother is not in a cold and dark grave. She is happy in heaven with God and her loved ones," Ms. Freeman says she was told. For information on the newsletter, write: AngelWatch, P.O. Box 1362, Mountainside NJ 07092.

**Angra Mainyu**. The chief spirit of evil in the former world religion of Zoroastrianism, today a minor sect. Zoroastrianism, the religion of the ancient Persian Empire, was the first major western religion to argue that good and bad angels are fighting invisibly behind the scenes. In this cosmic war, Ahura Mazda, the head spirit of goodness, continually does good deeds for the universe. But every time he does, his dark twin Angra Mainyu, the Zoroastrian devil, spitefully counters the good action with a corresponding, mirror-image evil deed. Among other misdeeds, Angra Mainyu caused man's original language to be divided into 30 tongues, from which today's languages have descended -- and he fatally poisoned the first man, Gayomart. And when Ahura Mazda made the stars of heaven, Angra Mainyu created the planets, whose harmful astrological influences plagued the earth.

**Anpiel**. An angel in charge of looking after birds, according to Jewish kabbalist mystics.

**Apollyon**. (The Destroyer) The righteous angel of hell's Bottomless Pit, as described in the Bible's *Book of Revelation*. During the end times, Apollyon will chain Satan and throw him into the Pit for a 1,000 years, locking him away with a key. According to Revelation, the Bottomless Pit will eventually be opened up in the end times to set free swarms of human-faced locusts who torture sinners for five months -- insects controlled by Apollyon.

(Demons, by the way, are also imprisoned in the Pit until Doomsday.) However, in writings outside of the Bible, Apollyon is usually considered a fallen angel -- some writers describing him as snake-like, writhing in a pit at the center of the seventh and lowest layer of hell.

**Apsara**. A cosmic being who entertains the gods with dancing, singing and sex, according to Hindu mythology. In other words, celestial courtesans. When these voluptuous water nymphs first appeared, neither the gods nor the demons would take them as wives, so they became hussies. Sometimes, the gods would send an apsara to earth to seduce, and therefore sidetrack, an evil man from his mischief. The apsaras also sometimes voluptuously embraced the newly dead as they carried them into the afterlife. Slain heroes, for example, enjoyed an electrifying time with the apsaras in the personal heaven of the thunder god Indra, a heavy drinking, strutting warrior who drove his sun-chariot across the sky each day. In certain Moslem folklore, there was a similar belief that a Moslem soldier who killed a Christian during a holy war would be rewarded in Paradise with two angelic females for his sensual pleasure.

**Aquinas, Thomas**. The greatest angel scholar of the Middle Ages, who has been dubbed the "Angelic Doctor." While still a student, Aquinas was called "Dumb Ox" by his classmates because he was heavyset and close-mouthed. But his teacher, Albertus Magnus, shot back: "This ox will one day fill the world with his bellowing."

Sure enough, Aquinas' Texas-sized *Summa Theologica* (See Summa Theologica) gives an excruciatingly detailed description of the angel life. A strange legend about Aquinas has an angel protecting his chastity with a magic girdle around his loins. The tale goes that Aquinas' mother was so dead set against his going into church work that she had him kidnaped and imprisoned in the family castle for more than a year. During that time, she sent a woman to seduce him, whom Thomas promptly threw out. But that night, an angel was said to have visited him, putting a mystical girdle around Thomas' hips to ensure against further temptation.

**Archangels**. Archangels once were considered the highest rank of angels. But in the early Middle Ages, when the Christian Church became enthusiastic about a new theory of angel rankings, the archangels suddenly became the second-lowest of nine orders of angels. The conflict between the new and old theories explains the rank confusion in today's angel squadrons, where, for example, Michael, the commander-in-chief of heaven's armies, only holds the lowly title of archangel. As theologian Geddes MacGregor observed in his *Angels: Ministers of Grace*: "Mightn't it even be almost like having a corporal in charge of the United States Army?" At any rate, today, archangels are believed to look after worldwide godly ideas, like the notion of worshipping God. Another job of theirs is to carry God's most important messages to the human race, as when the archangel Gabriel told Mary she would be the mother of Jesus. (See Pseudo-Dionysius)

**Art and Angels**. Over the centuries, Christians have created the lion's share of angel art for lack of much competition: Orthodox Judaism and Islam both have taboos against illustrating religious figures. Fortunately, the Orthodox branch of Christianity only bans *three-dimensional* representations, allowing its sanctuaries to be filled with two-dimensional icons.

In portraying angels, artists are dealing with the unseen and spiritual, and their tool for showing the unshowable is the symbol. For example, by the 400s A.D., the century when the Roman Empire was falling apart, artists had gotten into the habit of painting a halo or circle of light above the head of angels or saints to symbolize their virtue. (See Halo) Sometimes a star was used over the head or on the breast to show holiness. Other symbols have included:

■ A flaming sword. Angels enforcing God's judgment often were shown holding flaming swords (as the no-nonsense cherubs did who were posted at the Garden of Eden to keep the exiled Adam and Eve from getting back in).

■ Wings. Among other things, wings have symbolized the rapid (actually, instantaneous) movement of a spiritual being traveling at the speed of thought.

■ Harps and musical instruments. Angel choirs playing harps and other instruments have been a good symbol for the unearthly beautiful heavenly music reported by mystics and visionary saints (See Harps).

■ Trumpets. If carrying a message from God, the herald angel might be painted with a trumpet.

■ Lily. To show purity, the angel might be painted carrying a lily, as in the art works where Gabriel holds a lily when appearing before the Virgin Mary to announce that she will bear Christ.

Also, from time to time, artists have slipped into standardized ways of showing different ranks of angels. Thrones are often shown as fiery wheels because the prophet Ezekiel saw them that way. Archangels are frequently shown wearing armor or perhaps having sandals on their feet while the next lower rank, the guardian angels, are clad in robes and barefoot.

How far back in time does angel art go? Some scholars think the earliest known work of art showing an angel-like being is a stone engraving from the 4,000-year-old city of Ur (the city Abraham, the forefather of the Jewish race, left to begin his trek to the Promised Land) in the Persian Gulf area. On this stone slab, a winged being pours the "water of life" into a cup held by a Sumerian king. Since that time, the growing choirs of angel artists have included these standouts:

- Fra Angelico, who is among the greatest of the angel artists. He believed his art was divinely inspired and prayed before starting a project. His tender Renaissance angel art so impressed Michaelangelo that he said the paintings must have been based on actual heavenly visions.

- Albrecht Duerer, the most important of the German artists in general. His 17-woodcut Renaissance series, *The Apocalypse of John*, illustrates angel-populated scenes of Doomsday from the Bible's Book of Revelation.

- William Blake, the 18th Century visionary, who produced some of the greatest sheer volume of angel art, illustrating such angel-studded classics as Milton's *Paradise Lost* and Dante's *Divine Comedy*. Blake himself said he saw angels in trees as a boy.

Unappreciated in his day, he is now considered a genius. Said Blake: "The man who has never in his mind and thought traveled to heaven is not an artist."

Until the late 1600s, artists showed angels performing superhuman and momentous deeds, like stopping the torture of Christian martyrs. Most momentous of all in the eyes of Christian artists was the crucifixion scene which often abounded in angels. A famous crucifixion scene is Giotti's painting showing small, human-looking angels hovering near the Cross and tearing at their chests in despair. In many other paintings, angels fly around the Cross with cups to catch the blood pouring from Christ's wounded hands and side. In modern times, artists began showing angels doing homely things, like guiding the awkward steps of toddlers and protecting them as they sleep, notes Clara Clement in her book *Angels in Art*. Some of the most common angel activities shown in art, she adds, include: Musical angels, adoring angels, and mourning angels. In modern times -- until very recently -- angel art had declined hand-in-hand with the once waning interest in angels.

**Ashmedai**. He runs hell's casinos, by some mythological accounts. And, by others, was responsible for getting Noah intoxicated. According to the Book of Genesis, however, Noah needed no help. Genesis says Noah was a farmer, and after the Flood, he planted the world's first vineyard, then sampled the fruit of the vine. One Jewish legend adds that Noah had gotten the vinestock from the Garden of Eden before the Flood. After the Flood, the evil angel Samael, Noah's vineyard partner, secretly put under the growing vine the blood of a slain lion, pig and ape, so its roots would suck up the blood. Thus, to this day, if a timid man drinks a little wine, he soon moves confidently like a lion; drinking a little more than he should, he acts like a pig; even more, and he acts like a foolish, lurching ape and becomes brainless.

**Asmodeus**. In Bible legend, Asmodeus was a demon of drunkenness and lust who delighted in strangling bride grooms on their wedding night in the nuptial bedchamber. According to the *Book of Tobit*, a young man named Tobias was scheduled to marry an unfortunate widow who had lost seven previous grooms to this fiend. But Tobias had an advantage, since the angel Raphael had taken him under his wing, so to speak. On the way to meet his bride, the nervous Tobias was told by Raphael to cut open a fish he had caught and keep the heart, liver and gall for use against Asmodeus. The greasy combination worked. Asmodeus was disgusted by the smoke as Tobias burned the fish organs on his wedding night. The demon fled from the Persian bedchamber all the way to Egypt, where he was tied up by another angel.

**Azazel**. In ancient folklore, Azazel is one of 200 lustful angels who descended to earth to have sex with attractive mortal women -- thus falling from grace. Azazel compounded this offense against God by teaching forbidden knowledge. Helping him here was the angel Gadreel, who taught humans how to make weapons, as well as other fallen angels teaching similar forbidden subjects like the vanity of cosmetics and how to write. (See Semjaza) Azazel started out as the name of a vague Old Testament desert creature.

Each year, on the Day of Atonement, the Hebrew high priest sent this creature a scapegoat. But before dispatching the goat into the desert, the high priest symbolically loaded down the animal with all of Israel's sins for that year -- thus purifying the Jewish people. Eventually, Azazel became a fallen angel in the eyes of Hebrew mystics.

**Azrael.** The Islamic angel of death with four faces, who is covered with a million veils as he flies on four wings. If you could look under the veils, you would see a body completely covered with innumerable eyes -- one eye for each living person. Every time one of Azrael's eyes blinks, a mortal is dying somewhere in the world.

Azrael keeps a roster listing the names of all human beings, but he does not know when individual deaths will happen. When the time for a particular person's death has come, Allah lets a leaf drop from the tree below His Throne -- on which is written the name of the person to die. Azrael then reads the name and separates the soul from the person's body after 40 days. Sometimes a mortal resists the separation, though. To help things along, Azrael will sometimes fly back to Allah to get an enticing apple from Paradise to show the reluctant mortal.

According to one Islamic legend, Azrael got his job as the angel of death by helping Allah create Adam, the first man. According to this story, Allah had originally sent off the angels Djibril (Gabriel), Mikal (Michael) and Israfel -- not Azrael -- to earth on a mission to facilitate the creation. The trio was supposed to gather up different types of clay for Allah to use in making Adam.

However, the earth refused the soil, warning the angelic trio that the new creature would rebel against his Maker and bring misfortune to earth. Therefore, the trio came back to heaven without the variously colored soils. An unhappy Allah then turned to the hard-nosed Azrael to get the soil. Azrael wouldn't take any earthly no for an answer. In the end, Allah rewarded the determined Azrael for his successful mission by putting him in charge of the sometimes tough job of splitting off dying people's spirits from their bodies.

**Balberith**. Hell's secretary and archivist, according to medieval occultists. In the mythology, his jobs include notarizing the deals between mortals and the devil.

**Battlefield Angels**. Through the centuries, angels have been credited with being the "sword of the Lord," providing help to soldiers on the battlefield against their foes. And of course, God is usually on the side of the narrator of this kind of intervention story, which goes back a long way. In the Old Testament, for example, the Hebrew prophet Elisha and his servant found themselves surrounded by an Assyrian army. And since the Assyrians were the Nazis of the ancient Near East and enemies of Elisha's, the prophet's servant shouted: "We are doomed, sir!" But a calm Elisha uttered his famous words: "Those who are for us are more than those who are against us." At that point, the servant suddenly was able to see fiery angelic cavalry and chariots surrounding Elisha. After that, the Assyrian soldiers were blinded, according to this legend.

In modern times, Hans Moolenburgh in his *Handbook of Angels* recalls how the famous World War II general George Patton startled his staff during the Battle of the Bulge by suddenly striking up a conversation out loud with God in front of them. What prompted Patton's sudden talk with God? A little background: In late 1944, the Germans had taken advantage of snowfall and cloudy weather to launch a massive counter-offensive, knowing the cloud cover would keep the Allies from using their greatly superior air power. "I need four days of fine (clear) weather," the flamboyant Patton stated to the Lord, as his officers looked on. "Otherwise, I cannot be held responsible for the consequences." Patton's prayer was distributed on 300,000 Christmas cards. The skies, unexpectedly, did clear -- and for the four days Patton had requested. The Allied planes took to the air, and the Axis offensive was stopped.

**Beelzebub**. (Lord of the Flies) The New Testament mentions Beelzebub as the "prince of demons" -- as when Jesus' enemies accused him of being possessed by Beelzebub because Christ had the power to exorcize demons out of individuals. In the New Testament, Beelzebub is the same as Satan, but sometimes legends make him Satan's major lieutenant. In folklore, Beelzebub, along with Satan, had a face-off with Christ during the three days Christ's body stayed in the tomb before the resurrection. During that time, mythology has Christ storming the gates of hell, being tested by hellfire yet remaining unhurt. In the *Gospel of Nicodemus*, Christ, during his three days in hell, promoted Beelzebub to head devil in the sulphurous domain -- in the process demoting Satan.

**The Old Testament patriarch Jacob dreams of a staircase joining heaven and earth. (Gustav Dore illustration)**

Christ did so after Beelzebub had harshly criticized Satan for being stupid enough to set up Christ's crucifixion on earth. Satan had mistakenly figured that killing Christ would make him Satan's prisoner in hell forever. Instead, a powerful Christ, bathed in light, came down to hell, horrified the devils there, and set free all the pre-Christian "saints in prison" such as John the Baptist, King David and the Hebrew prophet Isaiah. Despite Satan's protests, Christ led these saints to heaven, where the archangel Michael turned them over to a committee of greeters -- the Hebrew prophet Elijah, the Old Testament patriarch Enoch, and the thief who repented on the Cross.

Beelzebub started out as a Canaanite god and eventually got the nickname "Lord of the Flies." In ancient times, there was a widespread idea that flies carried souls in them. If a woman swallowed a fly, the soul inside would enter her womb, impregnating her, according to author Malcolm Godwin. The nickname "Lord of the Flies" stuck because of Beelzebub's job of transporting Canaanite souls.

**Belief in Angels**. A 1978 Gallup poll showed that 54 per cent of Americans believed in angels, but belief was highest among the young. A 1988 Gallup survey found that 74 per cent of American teens believed. On the subject of belief in angels, Harold Begbie wrote in his 1915 *On the Side of the Angels*: "Not to believe in the angels is to believe in a mindless, meaningless and soulless universe -- is to believe in an achievement by blind and irrational forces of order, beauty and goodness; is to believe in a miracle infinitely more miraculous than the existence of God."

**Angels swarm in the heaven of the fixed stars.**
(Gustav Dore illustration for The Divine Comedy)

**Beliel** (Worthless). In Puritan John Milton's epic poem *Paradise Lost*, Beliel is a devil known for lewdness and reasonable-sounding lies. In occult mythology of the Middle Ages, Beliel was considered to be hell's ambassador to Turkey. Often, the name Beliel is used as just another name for Satan, as when Christianity's greatest missionary, Paul of Tarsus, writes in the New Testament, "How can Christ and Beliel agree?"

**Belphegor** (Lord of the Opening). The demon of inventiveness and also Hell's ambassador to France, according to Middle Ages occult myth. Belphegor may have earned the post because of his previous tenure as ancient Moab's lewd god of sexual abandon (Baalpeor). Naturally, by some accounts, he is the guardian devil of risque Paris. Once, according to legend, hell's devils were deeply disturbed to hear a rumor that there were some happily married couples on earth, and Belphegor was sent out on a fact-finding mission. "Belphegor's experiences during his search and the many things he saw that happened between married couples soon convinced him that the rumor was groundless," wrote author Fred Gettings in recounting the story.

**Bethelda**. The angel that Theosophical clairvoyant Geoffrey Hodson said contacted him. Hodson said Bethelda furnished revelations that he used in five books, including the 1927 *Brotherhood of Angels and Men*. Hodson contended that angels are divided into classes with specialized roles: angels of nature, angels of healing, angels of beauty and art, etc.

**Biblical Angels**. The word angel or angels appears around 200 times in the classic King James version of the Bible, according to *Cruden's Complete Concordance*. Some of the chief Biblical happenings involving angels are as follows:

■ God put two cherubim with flaming swords east of the Garden of Eden to prevent the banished Adam and Eve from returning.

■ An angel stayed the hand of Abraham as he was about to kill his young son Isaac as a sacrifice.

■ Abraham entertained angels without being aware of it.

■ Jacob wrestled with the Dark Angel at Peniel.

■ An angel blocked the soothsayer Balaam who was on his way to put a curse on Israel.

■ An angel slaughtered 185,000 Assyrian soldiers laying seige to Jerusalem.

■ An angel brought nourishment to the prophet Elijah.

■ Angels announced the birth of Christ to shepherds.

■ An angel consoled Christ during his pre-arrest agonizing in the Garden of Gethsemane.

■ An angel appeared to women who were visiting Christ's tomb after his crucifixion and resurrection.

■ An angel freed the apostle Peter from prison.

**Bodhisattva**. This is an angel-like mortal who has become so spiritual that he doesn't have to reincarnate on earth any longer to learn more lessons but can go on to a higher plane of existence, *Nirvana* (see Nirvana) according to Mahayana Buddhism. Nevertheless, because of his love, he freely chooses to go back to our earthly "veil of tears" to continue to help and guide the spiritually needy human race -- postponing his personal salvation.

Acting roughly like angels, the bodhisattvas have stored up, over hundreds of lifetimes, a huge reservoir of "religious merit" which they can freely transfer to lesser mortals to help their souls. In fact, the bodhisattva's self-sacrifice could be so great that he might decide to be born into one of the Buddhist hells to help the damned "see the light." According to the Nagarjuna brand of Buddhism, a bodhisattva is a mortal who has become so spiritual that he can't backslide morally or intellectually. If he chooses to reincarnate, he is destined to be born into a very favorable position because of his good karma and will come to be known for his wisdom and love. The Buddhists believe that anyone of any religion can become a bodhisattva. Great spiritual teachers or benevolent kings are viewed as possible bodhisattvas. And selfless people serving humanity are thought to be on their way to becoming bodhisattvas.

**Bodies of Angels**. Medieval philosophers had two major views about the nature of angel bodies. One group, championed by the "Angelic Doctor" Thomas Aquinas, argued that angels were holy minds without bodies -- completely non-material spirits. Others, like Duns Scotus and his Scholastic followers, felt that angels do have bodies, but composed of a finer, subtler matter normally invisible to the eye. Interestingly, persons brushing with death and coming back to talk about what they felt was the afterlife offer both types of descriptions for their bodies. In her book *Messengers of Light*, Terry Lynn Taylor quotes a young boy uttering a short sentence that just might settle this debate: "Oh, they're just plain old air!" the youth noted.

**Chain of Being Argument**. For centuries, various leading philosophers have used this argument to try to prove, with logic alone, that an angelic kingdom ought to exist. The argument goes like this: All of creation is like a vast staircase with a huge number of steps upward. Every conceivable, tiny step on that staircase upward is filled with advancing life -- from the simplest creatures up to the human race. Is it reasonable, then, to assume that this ascending staircase of increasingly advanced life just breaks off abruptly with humans, making us the pinnacle of creation? If so, that would leave a huge gap, a yawning chasm, between man and God. This argument was popular with outstanding thinkers ranging from Thomas Aquinas, Roman Catholicism's greatest theologian, to John Locke, whose political ideas were borrowed by the Founding Fathers for our Declaration of Independence.

**Chamuel**. (One Who Sees God) Chamuel is one of several angels believed by different groups to be the dark angel (See Dark Angel) who wrestled with Jacob as well as the unnamed angel who comforted the agonized Christ in Jerusalem's Garden of Gethsemane just before his arrest (although some say the latter was Gabriel).

**Children**. The idea that the innocence and purity of children is a holdover from the heavenworld they have supposedly left to incarnate on earth (as some argue) is an old one. As the romantic poet of the 1800s William Wordsworth put it in his famous *Ode on Intimations of Immortality*: "Our birth is but a sleep and a forgetting./ The Soul that rises with us, our life's Star/ Hath had elsewhere its setting,/ And cometh from afar;/ Not in entire forgetfulness,/ And in utter nakedness,/ But trailing clouds of glory do we come/ From God who is our home:/ Heaven lies about us in our infancy!" Or as Jesus noted, "See that you don't despise any of these little ones. Their angels in heaven, I tell you, are always in the presence of my Father in heaven." Perhaps children's innocence, wherever it comes from, contributes to the fact that they seem to see angels more often. In fact, there is a category of angel encounter stories in which children have seen angels in a critical moment when the adults around them missed the vision. Consider this account in the December 1992 *Ladies' Home Journal* (names in the following story were changed): Carole Moore's eighteen-month-old daughter, Allison, stopped breathing. Holding the limp child in her arms as the toddler's lips turned blue, the frantic mother went into the hallway of her apartment building, screaming for help. But no one answered her. Then, however, a great feeling of peacefulness came over the mother. "Relax, Carole," the mother said to herself. "You took a class in child safety last year. You know what to do." Carole could visualize herself doing what had to be done. Elder daughter Julie, just shy of three years old, looked on as her mother gave her toddler sister mouth-to-mouth resuscitation. Allison resumed her breathing. Later, a doctor diagnosed Allison's sickness as croup. That evening, Julie was on her mother's lap when she said: "Mommy, who was that man who had his hand on your shoulder." Carole asked Julie what man? Julie told her mother that she saw a man laying his hand on Carole's shoulder as Carole was resuscitating Allison -- a man invisible to Carole.

In a similar vein, Melvin Morse reports in his *Closer to the Light* how a heavily armed family took 150 children hostage at a school in Cokesville, Wyoming in 1986. And yet, despite a bomb being set off, no child was harmed, even though the entire school was destroyed. A large number of children claimed they saw glowing people who helped them get to safe places before the bomb detonated. As an example, Morse quotes one girl as saying that the luminous beings she saw and heard were hovering above her: "The woman (one of the entities) told us that a bomb was going off soon and to listen to our brother. They were dressed in white, like light bulbs, but brighter around the face. The woman made me feel good. I knew she loved me." Meanwhile, the girl's brother, although he saw nothing, claimed to have heard a voice telling him to find his little sister, take her to a particular window and make sure she stayed there.

**Cherubim**. The second-highest rank of angels in the Catholic Church's traditional belief. The cherubim are often pictured as full of eyes to symbolize their great intellect. They are heaven's "detail men" -- helping to conceive the particulars of what is to be done to carry out the Divine Plan, according to the popular Dionysian theory traditionally embraced by the Catholic Church. In angel lore, the cherubim are God's record keepers. In popular opinion, cherubs have gone from being thought of 3,000 years ago as monstrous winged lions with human heads guarding ancient buildings to being drawn today as chubby winged babes on Christmas cards -- a fascinating evolution.

In Bible lore, cherubs show up in their role as place guards at the Garden of Eden with flaming swords -- to keep the banished Adam and Eve away from the Garden's Tree of Life. (See Pseudo-Dionysius)

**Clarence Oddbody**. Perhaps one of the most famous angels in modern cinema. Clarence is the lisping, bumbling angel who saves George Bailey (Jimmy Stewart) when he tries to commit suicide by jumping off a bridge in the classic 1946 movie *It's a Wonderful Life*. Stewart's character, who'd been a lifelong positive thinker and selfless helper of any and all, was suddenly facing bankruptcy and had become suicidal and negative on Christmas Eve. Clarence, on the other hand, was a 292-year-old "angel second class." For centuries, junior angel Clarence had been trying unsuccessfully to earn his wings, and now, he had a golden opportunity to make it happen by straightening out Stewart's protagonist. So, when the disgusted and despondent Bailey wished to Clarence that he'd never been born, Clarence obliged. He showed Bailey what a miserable town his happy Bedford Falls would have become had he never lived to love the people there and sacrifice for them. This vision turns Bailey around, and he then learns that the townfolk have taken up a massive collection to save him from financial ruin. Clarence vanishes, but he leaves Bailey a goodbye note: "Remember: No man is a failure who has friends."

**Coincidence**. "When I pray," said an Anglican archbishop, "coincidences happen. When I cease to pray, they stop happening."

Angels and higher benevolent powers are commonly believed to benefit mortals by setting up helpful or instructive coincidences. As one observer put it, "Coincidence is God's way of performing a miracle anonymously." A case in point: In 1799, a depressed William Cowper decided to drown himself in London's Thames River. But his taxicab became lost in fog, the cabbie, unbeknownst to Cowper, wandered aimlessly through the streets. Finally, the cabbie admitted to Cowper that he could not even get his fare back home again. Cowper stepped out of the carriage, moved through the thick mist and suddenly realized he was back at his front door! In response to this incredible coincidence, Cowper wrote a hymn still commonly sung today: *God Moves in Mysterious Ways His Wonders to Perform*. Cowper's brush with coincidence on a day of literal and figurative fog is not unique to him. As the Dutch surgeon Hans Moolenburgh, author of *A Handbook of Angels*, put it: "If you watch carefully, you can see 'coincidence' continually at work in your life, right down to the small and unimportant details."

**Conferences among Angels**. In his book *The Many Faces of Angels*, Harvey Humann notes that Pope Pius XI mentioned to visitors once that if he was about to speak with someone who might be unfriendly to his message, he would request that his guardian angel confer with the guardian angel of other person to smooth things out. Pius said his conversation with the potential antagonist would then go on without turmoil.

**Constellations**. Today's sky atlas of constellations swarms with the colorful heros, maids and monsters from Greek and Roman mythology, such as the Great Bear (Ursa Major, i.e. the Big Dipper), which is a mortal woman who had an affair with Zeus and was changed into a bear because of wife Hera's jealousy but put in the sky afterward by Zeus, the king of the gods, who cared for her nevertheless. Despite the near- Greco-Roman monopoly on today's sky, some angelic stories from Judaeo-Christian tradition have also been part of constellation folklore in times past, according to scholar Richard Hinckley Allen in his *Star Names: Their Lore & Meaning*. The ancient Jews, for example, called today's prominent classical Greek constellation Orion (often one of the first that stargazers learn) by the name *Gibbor* (the Giant) and considered it to be the inescapable Biblical hunter Nimrod. Nimrod was thought by some to be the son of a fallen angel and the builder of the Tower of Babel, eventually hung in heaven by Yahweh as punishment for trying to storm heaven. (See Nimrod) Some medievals considered the zodiac constellation Virgo the Virgin to represent the Virgin Mary, queen of the angels, holding the baby Jesus.

From time to time, certain star atlas makers and constellation designers have tried (unsuccessfully) to "sanctify" the star map by replacing the Greco-Roman star patterns with Bible-oriented constellations -- an effort that peaked in the 1600s. Among other things, some of these mapmakers took Draco the Dragon, a classical monster whirled by the goddess of wisdom Minerva into the sky, and turned it into the serpent who tempted Eve in the Garden of Eden. The so-called Biblical School of atlas makers also tinkered with the constellation Hydra the Water Snake, a dragon guarding the Golden Fleece that Jason and Argonauts sought. The water snake was turned into a new constellation, the Biblical Flood. And Hydra's companion constellation, Corvus the Crow (a silver crow punished by the Greek god Apollo, who turned him and his descendants black) was metamorphosed into Noah's Raven -- one of the birds Noah sent off from the ark to see if the floodwaters had receded enough to expose land. Mapmaker Julius Schiller turned the Great Bear (Big Dipper) into the archangel Michael, and he merged the constellations Hydrus and Tucana as well as the Lesser Megellanic Cloud (a nearby galaxy) and created the constellation Raphael the Archangel.

**Creation of Angels**. The traditional Christian belief is that eternal God was alone in the beginning. Then, He created angels, next the universe, and finally, humankind. However, some early Jewish writers thought that God creates angels every time he breathes. One rabbi wrote poetically that an angel is created every time a word comes out of God's mouth. Some mystics hold that a strong belief in an angel can create one out of God's energy.

**Dante**. This Middles Ages writer -- Italy's number one poet -- is literature's most famous tourist of heaven, purgatory and hell. In his fictional *Divine Comedy*, Dante was guided by the famous pagan Roman poet Virgil when Dante began his trip through the three realms by going down to hell. As the two passed through the gates of hell, they saw a sign reading: "Abandon hope all ye who enter in."

Hell is shaped like an inverted cone lined with layers. The highest layer is Limbo, where the unbaptized live without pain, except that they never see God. Here, in a circle of light, the two travelers found the great pagan, pre-Christian poets and philosophers living in a castle.

Dante and Virgil next climbed down to lower layers containing wrongdoers, each assigned to his place of torment by Minos, the Infernal Judge (See Minos). With each loss of altitude, the sins got worse. At the highest sinning level were the shrieking, lustful lovers violently blown about in a screeching wind. On levels below them were the gluttons, the misers and angry hotheads, each with similarly appropriate punishments. Further down, the heretics, the violent ones, and the con artists. The violent were kept submerged in a river of boiling blood by armed centaurs; flatterers were kept buried in excrement.

Cocytus, the lowest part of hell, contained traitors, and at the very lowest point in the universe was a gigantic Satan, the cosmic traitor who rebelled against his Benefactor -- caked waist-deep in a lake of ice (symbolizing the coldness of his lack of love). Satan's three faces each constantly were chewing on one of the three greatest sinners in the world: The betrayer of Jesus, Judas Iscariot, and the two betrayers of the Roman dictator Julius Caesar, Brutus and Cassius.

Leaving Satan behind, Virgil and Dante moved through a rock opening to pass through the center of the earth and begin moving upward again toward the surface of the southern hemisphere. Back on the surface, they climbed Mount Purgatory. The purgatory mountain is a well-organized school for *purging* (hence, "purgatory") stained souls of the seven deadly sins to prepare them for heaven. Here, the gluttonous, for example, were virtual skeletons from thirst and starvation; the greedy were forced to keep their eyes riveted to the ground, because on earth they were concerned only with earthly things.

At the peak of Mount Purgatory, Virgil and Dante reached the Garden of Eden, and Virgil said his goodbyes. As a non-Christian pagan, he was not allowed to go into the sky, where heaven lies. Dante was joined by his deceased love, Beatrice, who led him through the nine heavens -- the Moon (home of the good-intentioned), Mercury (abode of ambitious souls), Venus (amorous people), the Sun (realm of the wise), Mars (virtuous warriors), Jupiter (the just, including benevolent kings), Saturn (spiritual thinkers and contemplators), and, then, the second highest heaven -- the heaven of the fixed stars. To get there, Dante climbed Jacob's Ladder and entered the constellation Gemini, the sign of his birth. Dante met Jesus, the Virgin Mary, and the Apostles. Adam showed up and told Dante he lived 930 years on earth but another 4,032 in Limbo -- even though he had been in the blissful Garden of Eden just six hours before being kicked out for eating the forbidden fruit.

Dante next climbed to the ninth and highest heaven, where time and space stopped. Past the ninth heaven, Dante discovered that there is only an intelligent Light that is filled with Love for what is good. As Dante gazed on the Divine Light, he saw that every part of the Universe is tied together by spiritual love.

**Daimon**. Standing between the gods and man in status, the daimon was sometimes a guardian spirit in the ancient Greek philosophies of Stoicism and Neoplatonism. Actually, the daimon could either protect an individual or punish him for angering the gods. One of history's best known daimons was the one the famous ancient Greek philosopher Socrates claimed to have. According to legend, Socrates said his personal guardian spirit warned him of trouble ahead of time but never bossed him. On one occasion, this never-erring spirit supposedly cautioned Socrates against turning a particular corner. When his friends ignored the philosopher and rounded the corner, anyway -- they were suddenly shaken up and knocked down by a group of pigs. Plato believed that the guardian daimon gets stronger as a person seeks wisdom and spirituality; weaker if he pursues foolish and trivial things. Eventually, the daimon's double-edged job of bringing good or evil became separated. Good daimons developed into the modern idea of guardian angels, while malevolent daimons came to be thought of as demons or devils (the term demon comes from the word daimon).

**Dark Angel**. This is the mysterious supernatural being that the ancient Hebrew patriarch Jacob encountered and then wrestled with on the shore of the River Jabbok -- a tale found in the Old Testament's Book of Genesis. The grappling continued through the predawn hours. The strange being was getting the worst of it, but he hit Jacob on the hip, throwing it out of joint. Then, as the time for daybreak approached, the being became desperate to get away.

But Jacob would not release his grip on the dark angel until the entity agreed to bless him. Besides giving a blessing, the dark angel also changed Jacob's name. The entity said: "You have struggled with God and with men, and you have won; so your name will be Israel (Hebrew: "God Struggles")." Afterward, it was Jacob's turn to do the naming: He called the area Peniel, which means "I have seen God face-to-face and am still alive." In his *Dictionary of Angels*, angel scholar Gustav Davidson recalls a time when a supernatural being got physical with him in a similar way: "At this stage of the (angel research), I was literally bedeviled by angels. They stalked and leagured me by night and day..." At dusk one winter's day, Davidson said, he was cutting across an unfamiliar field on his way home from a neighbor's farm when suddenly "a nightmarish shape loomed up in front of me, barring my progress." For a moment paralyzed, Davidson finally fought his way past the "phantom." "The next morning I could not be sure (no more than Jacob was when he wrestled with his dark antagonist at Peniel) whether I had encountered a ghost, an angel, a demon or God," Davidson concluded.

**Death Angel of Sennacherib's Army**. The unnamed angel that saved the southern half of ancient Israel from being destroyed by Assyrian invaders, according to Bible legend. Here's what happened: The ancient religious reformer King Hezekiah of Judah (the southern kingdom of Israel) made a foreign policy blunder in 705 B.C. by joining an alliance of countries defying the awesomely powerful Assyrian Empire, that brutal Nazi-like war machine that dominated much of the ancient Middle East. Four years later, the Assyrian Emperor Sennacherib beat the coalition on the battlefield. Judah managed to survive by buying off the emperor's anger with a steep payment of tribute. (And a lucky thing, too, because a few years earlier, in 721 B.C., the Assyrians had already destroyed the northern kingdom of Israel and deported its population to other lands, where they mixed racially and lost their identity -- becoming the so-called "Ten Lost Tribes.") But despite Hezekiah's hefty tribute, things heated up again around 690 B.C. when the Assyrian Emperor Sennacherib sent a large army to lay seige to Jerusalem. According to Bible legend, a grieving Hezekiah tore his clothes and put on the customary sackcloth, but the prophet Isaiah told the king not to worry. Hezekiah's prayers in the Temple had been answered, Isaiah declared, and he quoted God as saying poetically to Sennacherib, "I will put a hook through your nose and a bit in your mouth, and take you back by the same road you came." Soon after, according to this legend, an unnamed angel went to the Assyrian camp and slaughtered 185,000 soldiers, forcing the Assyrians to retreat. Historically speaking, some scholars suspect it was actually an outbreak of plague that routed the Assyrians.

**Deathbed Visions**. Dying persons often seem to develop the ability to peer into the spiritual world, while still lingering among the living -- particularly in their last moments. With a foot each in two worlds, the dying often claim that close loved ones who preceded them in death or religious figures are appearing to them, saying they are preparing to escort them into the next world.

To give a personal example: A few days before she died in the 1980s, a great-aunt of mine announced that her father, dead since the 1930s, had visited her and told her he would be coming for her. Parapsychologists call these figures "take-away apparitions," and these apparitions include beings of light, which some consider angels. In his book *Deathbed Visions*, William Barrett related the case of two young children, close friends, dying of diphtheria in the 1880s, Jennie and Edith. Jennie died first, but the news was kept from Edith. But three days after Jennie's death, Edith was claiming that her friend had come to her bedside. "Why, Papa, I am going to take Jennie with me!" she exclaimed. "Oh, Jennie, I'm so glad you are here." She held out her arms into the thin air and died a short time later. Occasionally, persons who are part of the deathbed vigil report seeing a take-away apparition. Sometimes also, witnesses claim to see the life essence of the dying person hovering above the physical body as a cloud of energy which finally fades. In a large minority of cases, the deathbed vision also includes a prevision of the next world, often of gorgeous afterlife scenery, such as beautiful landscapes and vegetation.

**Demiurge** (Ancient Greek: "Worker for the People"). In the ancient religion of gnosticism -- a major world religion during the time of the Roman Empire and a strong rival of young, growing Christianity -- the demiurge was the weak, ignorant and perverse angel who created and ruled the physical world, a world considered evil and without God's presence.

(The gnostics believed that the good God was too high up in the upper heavens to pay attention to our lower physical world of matter, which was at the mercy of the demiurge.) In Ophite gnostic mythology, for example, the demiurge is Ialdabaoth, who poses as Yahweh, the Israelite God of the Old Testament. Ialdabaoth creates Adam, but then grows jealous of the first man's huge size and shining body. So he decides to "cut Adam down to size" by creating Eve. However, the cosmic Feminine Principle counterattacks against Ialdabaoth by sending the Serpent to Eden to get Adam and Eve to eat the forbidden fruit so they can get knowledge of heavenly Virtue and reject their evil creator. The testy Ialdabaoth then kicks Adam and Eve out of Paradise, located in one of the lower heavens -- down to earth. Eventually, Christ incarnates on earth, teaching humans even more heavenly knowledge which Ialdabaoth would like to keep from them. Ialdabaoth and his lower angels, called *archons*, retaliate by scheming to get Jesus executed on a cross. But Jesus ends up sitting at the right hand of an ignorant Ialdabaoth, secretly helping Perfect souls escape the lower heavens to the higher ones populated by God and the good angels -- all of this right under Ialdabaoth's nose. Ialdabaoth would like every human soul to reincarnate endlessly on earth and stay his prisoner in the physical world. This story shows how the gnostics had a strange habit of turning the Old Testament heros into villains and vice-versa. Gnostics were especially mistrustful of the Old Testament god Yahweh, who they felt was an imposter of the actual, good God higher up, with Ialdabaoth showing his true colors by his brutality in the Bible (acting under the name Yahweh).

The guardian angel of a mourner tries to tell him his dead friend is at rest in heaven. (William Blake illustration)

The gnostic imagination cultivated a jungle of contradictory mythologies, and so the identity of the demiurge varied from gnostic sect to gnostic sect.

**Devils**. Some ancient Jews believed that demons sprang from the bodies of a race of evil giants drowned during the Flood -- giants begotten by fallen angels who mated with mortal women. The demons then continued to plague the earth indefinitely. Other rabbis thought that God created them. Christians traditionally have believed that devils are the bad angels who followed Satan in his rebellion against God during the War in Heaven and were thrown down to hell (See War in Heaven). Christian medievals often believed that devils are stupid, frightened of church bells, mortal, and can take any shape they want. Unlike angels, devils can reproduce, but their lifespans are short, the thinking went. Ancient and medieval Christians also had a habit of turning pagan gods and godlings into devils. Celtic Christians, for example, contended that the fairies were the children of fallen angels. Some medieval occultists convinced themselves that devils were organized into an "infernal empire," consisting of such feudal ranks as princes and dukes, and even a prime minister, all of them subject to Beelzebub. In this elaborate mythology, certain devils were engaged as "ambassadors" to particular nations. Before the 1100s, the Church did not believe that demons could have sex with humans. Two centuries later, though, this idea had become an official belief. Demons acting like men, called *incubi* (Latin: "To lie upon"), were believed to attack women, while demons looking like women, called *succubi* (Latin: "To lie under"), preyed on men.

**Djahannam**. The moslem hell, a place of boiling water and pus where infidels are roasted. For moslems, it is usually thought to be a temporary place of purification. Djahannam is overseen by the righteous but fearsome angel Malik. (See Malik)

**Djibril**. The moslem version of the archangel Gabriel. On the "Night of Power and Glory," an Arabic-speaking Djibril came to the prophet Mohammed and dictated to him the heavenly copy of the Koran. Djibril was an awesome sight. His green wings spanned much of the horizon, and between the two eyes of his shining face were written the words: "There is no God but God, and Mohammed is the Prophet of God." With Djibril guiding him, Mohammed mounted a magical mule with wings and a woman's face called the *Buraq* ("Lightning") and flew off into the night with Gabriel. Then: Stepping off the top of one of Islam's holiest shrines, the Dome of the Rock (which stands on the ruins of the Second Jewish Temple), Mohammed climbed a golden ladder to ascend to the various heavens, running into Isa (Jesus) and Idris (Hermes), Moses, Abraham and Adam, and the archangel Mikel (Michael). Mohammed finally entered a huge ocean of golden light, where he received knowledge of the divine -- before returning to earth. Among other duties in Moslem folklore, Djibril comforted Adam after his fall from grace, taught the first man the civilized arts, and even took him to the Moslem holy city Mecca to teach him the rites involved in making pilgrimages. In muslim legend, Djibril has 600 or more wings and the sun interposed between his eyes.

**Dominions**. The fourth-highest of the nine orders of angels in the Catholic Church's traditional belief. The dominions are heaven's executives, order-givers. They decide what needs to be done to accomplish God's cosmic goals, including giving orders necessary for the day-to-day workings of the universe. The dominions get their direction from the cherubim (See Cherubim, Also Pseudo-Dionysius).

**Dubbiel**. The guardian angel of the massive Persian Empire and a major player in ancient geopolitics, according to Jewish legend. Ancient Jews believed that the rise and fall of nations was decided by the countries' national guardian angels. These national angels struggled with one another in heaven, either actually fighting or just competing with each other to get influence with God, who would make decisions about countries' destinies. If a national angel won a heavenly struggle with another national angel, the victor angel's country would triumph on earth over the beaten angel's country. For example, the great expansion of the ancient Persian Empire, the largest empire the world had ever seen in its day, the 500s through the 300s B.C., was believed to come from the heavenly work of the guardian angel of Persia, Dubbiel. Legend says Dubbiel pulled off this coup when he temporarily bumped the pro-Israel Gabriel from his job in God's inner sanctum. The whole story had begun when God, angry with Israel, had decided to totally wipe out Israel with hot coals from under the Almighty's chariot. The dirty work fell to an unwilling Gabriel. Gabriel fudged by dilly-dallying, letting a laggard cherub hand him the coals, knowing that the coals were cooling off because of the delay.

As a result, down on earth, the Babylonian army under King Nebuchadnezzer indeed ravaged Israel, destroyed the First Temple and smashed Jerusalem, but did not completely wipe out the Jewish race. However, Jewish nobles were carried off as hostages into the Babylonian Captivity to make sure there'd be no more uprisings. When God realized his plan had been foiled by Gabriel, he kicked Gabriel out of his inner circle, replacing him with Persia's Dubbiel. With his new influential post next to the Throne, Dubbiel lost no time seeing to it that, on earth, great gobs of land were conquered by Persia. After 21 days, though, Gabriel finessed Dubbiel by sticking his head briefly inside the curtain surrounding God, Dubbiel and the other insiders -- and reminded the Lord about how righteous the Jewish prophet Daniel had been. This got Gabriel restored to the heavenly throne room at Dubbiel's expense. The entire legend is cited by Bernard J. Bamberger in his scholarly *Fallen Angels*.

**Eden**. In the Bible's Book of Genesis, Eden is the name of a region where God planted a beautiful garden for Adam and Eve "in the East." The word Eden comes from the ancient Sumerian language where it just meant "plain." In the middle of the garden was one tree that gave life and another tree with fruit that would give a person knowledge to know right from wrong. It was the latter tree whose fruit Adam and Eve ate, disobeying God's command. Out of the garden flowed a river which split into four streams, the Tigris and Euphrates Rivers, and the Pishon and Gihon Rivers (possibly ancient names for the Nile River and Persian Gulf).

In Puritan John Milton's multi-volume poem *Paradise Lost*, Adam, before he sinned by eating the forbidden fruit, was able to talk freely in the Garden of Eden with God and angels. In the Garden, he spent his time as a caretaker and also gave animals their names. One day, Satan entered the body of a serpent and caught Eve alone. The serpent told her that he had learned to speak and had become wise because he ate fruit from the forbidden Tree of Knowledge. Eve then ate the fruit, with Adam following her lead. After the Fall of Man -- Sin and Death, preparing to come to Earth for the first time, built a wide road to Earth over Chaos, the chaotic space between heaven, earth and hell. A despairing Eve was ready to commit suicide, but Adam told her that the archangel Michael predicted that one of her descendants, Jesus Christ, would one day wipe out their offense against God.

In the mythical *First Book of Adam and Eve*, Adam was frightened when, after being kicked out of the Garden of Eden, the darkness of night was introduced into the world -- in contrast to the eternal day of Eden. The trauma of the first night was followed by the shock of the first morning when a scared Adam and Eve watched the first sunrise, thinking the sun was a fiery God coming to burn them. To console and comfort the primordial couple, God sent Michael to fetch glowing golden rods from the Indian Ocean area, and Gabriel and Raphael to get incense and myrrh from the Garden of Eden. The angels brought the three Christmas-style gifts to Adam and Eve. The glowing gold was particularly helpful because at night it lit their gloomy home, the Cave of Treasures.

Other problems that cropped up as a result of the Fall of Man, according to general folklore: God introduced harsh hot and cold seasons, in contrast to the climate-controlled Eden, and animals began eating each other.

**Electronic Angels**. Angels, it seems, are not averse to taking advantage of modern electronics to get their message across. Here is one incident described in Joan Wester Anderson's *Where Angels Walk*: At Asheville, N.C., pilot Henry Gardner's Cessna 180 aircraft encountered a solid blanket of fog shrouding the airport -- preventing any visual landing. Yet an air traffic controller told the light plane that the airport was not equipped to handle instrumental landings. The plane would have to go back to Greenville, S.C., to land, the controller said. Impossible, Gardner replied. His plane was almost out of fuel. There was silence from the controller. Then, he said curtly: "Okay. We'll get the ground crew ready. Come in on an emergency landing. During the plane's first blind descent, a voice suddenly exclaimed over the radio: "Pull it up! Pull it up!" Gardner lifted the plane, and then noticed through a break in fog that, thanks to the radio voice, he had just missed crashing into a bridge at an interstate highway.

On the next blind descent, the plane almost struck treetops before rising again. Then, the radio voice reappeared and gave Gardner detailed, minute instructions on how to maneuver the plane this way and that as it descended a third time. Finally, the voice said: "You're right over the end of the runway. Set it down... now!" After the plane landed, Gardner thanked the controller for probably saving his life.

The controller was taken aback: "What are you talking about? We lost all radio contact with you when we told you to return to Greenville." The controller added that he was stunned to see the light plane drop through the fog to the runway. Who had taken over radio communication and given landing instructions?"

Angels may not be the only ones on the other side using modern circuitry. One of the famous parapsychologist D. Scott Rogo's most popular books, *Phone Calls From the Dead* (co-authored with the noted psychical researcher Raymond Bayless), recounted how departed mortals allegedly have used Ma Bell to reach out and touch someone on this end, generally loved ones. In such cases, the caller supposedly is trying to pass on a warning, just say goodbye or provide other information. The calls usually take place shortly after the death of the caller.

**Enoch**. See Metatron.

**Erelim**. Gigantic angels watching over vegetation from the third heaven, and well-equipped to observe and report, since each has 70,000 heads, each head 70,000 mouths, each mouth 70,000 tongues, and each tongue 70,000 sayings, according to Ginzberg's *The Legends of The Jews*.

**Ethiopic Book of Enoch**. An ancient book swarming with named angels, penned by an author pretending to be the ancient righteous Bible patriarch Enoch. Many ancient Jews and Christians believed that Enoch was snatched up to heaven by God without having to suffer a physical death -- thanks to a few cryptic words in the Book of Genesis about God "taking" him.

As an added bonus, Enoch was turned into the fiery angel Metatron. (See Metatron) Actually written in stages around 100 B.C., this mythological tome talks about how the heaven-bound Enoch runs into a massive number of angels in charge of different natural forces, visits imprisoned fallen angels waiting for Doomsday, and learns about things that will happen in the end times. The book was very popular in ancient times, some early Christian church fathers considered it part of the Bible, and even today Ethiopian Orthodox Christians consider this book to be scripture. Here's a sampling of Enochian angels: Bardiel, the angel of lightning; Zakkiel, the angel of storms; Zamiel, the angel of hurricanes; Ruhiel, the angel of wind; Rashiel, the angel of cyclones and tornados; Zafiel, the angel of showers; Ramiel, the angel of thunder; Matriel, the angel of rain; Shalgiel, the angel of snow; Leliel, the angel of night; Shamshiel, the angel of day; Ofaniel, the angel of the moon; Kokabiel, the angel of the stars; Rahtiel, the angel of constellations; and Suiel, the angel of earthquakes.

**Ethnarchs**. After God disrupted the building of the 70-mile-high Tower of Babel by scattering humankind into different countries and confusing their one language into many, He appointed 70 angels closest to his Throne to be the guardian angels of the earth's new nations. These national angels were called *ethnarchs*. However, except for the guardian angel of righteous Israel, Michael -- all of the other national ethnarchs became too biased toward their Gentile countries, fell and became evil. True, God had ordered the ethnarchs of such ancient superpowers as Babylonia and Assyria to punish his sinful chosen people the Jews from time to time, but Babylonia and Assyria went way overboard. Among the fallen eth-narchs were Dubbiel (Persia) and Rahab (Egypt). Also, the Hebrew Enoch manuscript identifies Samael as the guardian angel of the Roman Empire, which held ancient Israel under its imperialistic rule. In one tradition, Rome's Samael has one long hair in his navel, and as long as this hair stays intact, Samael's evil rule will continue. But when the Jewish Messiah appears to free Israel from Rome, that hair will be bent as the loud blast of the shofar horn is heard. And as the hair bends, Samael -- and presumably Rome -- will collapse. In his book *Angels*, author Peter Lamborn Wilson notes that Portugal has been the only country to have a formal feast day in honor of its national guardian angel -- on the third Sunday in July.

**Fallen Angels**. All told, there are as many versions of how the bad angels fell as there are theories of how dinosaurs became extinct or why Rome collapsed. Here's a sampler:

■ In one ancient Jewish scenario, some of heaven's choir members eyed lovely mortal women, were overcome with lust, and defiled their holiness by having intercourse. This forbidden sex sired a race of terrible half-breed giants that plagued the earth. For their misdeeds, the angels fell and received terrible divine punishment. (See Semjaza, Mastema.)

■ In another version, Origen of Alexandria, probably the leading Biblical scholar of the ancient Christian church, believed that whether a being is an angel, human or devil depends on how far it decided to drift away from God's presence.

Origen contended that in the beginning, God created angel intelligences to stay with him and contemplate him. But God gave them the free will to thwart his plan if they wanted to. Some intelligences freely chose to stay close to God, according to plan. They became the highest angels, having ethereal bodies. Others wandered farther away and became lower angels, also with ethereal bodies. Still other beings strayed an even greater distance, becoming physical, fleshly human beings. Those who moved out the farthest became devils, with even coarser, cold bodies.

■ One of the most popular explanations is that an arrogant Satan, one of the highest angels, led a rebellion in heaven to take God's place, was defeated and thrown out of the sky, along with his followers. The Bible's Book of Revelation talks about the tail of the dragon (Satan) dragging a third of the stars of the sky (one third of the heavenly host) down with him to damnation. (See War in Heaven).

The famous Pope Gregory the Great and many other ancient Christians believed that God created mankind to replace the fallen angels. In the end, the number of saved souls going to heaven would exactly equal the number of fallen angels kicked out of the clouds. In 1273, the number of hooligan angels was reckoned, somehow, by the medieval Cardinal Bishop of Tusculum to be precisely 133,306,668, while the good angel count stood at 266,613,336. Some ancient authors, by the way, felt that shooting stars are fallen angels.

Is the grace of the good angels and the damnation of the fallen ones something sealed for eternity? Reasonable minds have differed.

The medieval philosopher Thomas Aquinas, one of the Catholic Church's greatest theologians, provides the traditional, orthodox Christian viewpoint: Good angels are eternally blessed and bad ones eternally damned. Aquinas believed that at the dawn of time, God gave all his angels a little window of opportunity, a brief period of free will, to accept or reject him. Once they cast their lot, the matter was settled forever. However, dissenters include Origen of Alexandria, one of the greatest Biblical scholars among the ancient church fathers, known for his unorthodox views. Origen felt that even good angels are capable of backsliding, as can humans who are not morally vigilant.

**Fioretti**. A written, diary-like collection of times in one's life when an angel intervened.

**Forbidden Knowledge**. The corruption of the young human race was furthered by fallen angels who fornicated with mortal women and also passed on to humankind forbidden knowledge, according to ancient Jewish legend. The angel Semyaza (See Semyaza) taught mortals how to exorcize evil spirits; Kawkabel taught them astrology; Ezekeel taught humans how to tell the future by watching the clouds; Armaros tutored them in casting spells.

**Foreign Expressions Concerning Angels**. A number of foreign phrases concerning angels have come into use in English. One of the more common is the Latin expression *Qui angelorum socius est*, meaning "... who is a companion (or partner) of the angels." This is usually used to describe a person, as in: John Doe, qui angelorum socius est.

A different foreign expression -- *ange passe* -- comes from French and means, "An angel is passing." This is said when there is a sudden lull in the middle of a conversation.

**Frashkart**. (The Final Rehabilitation) The final purging of all evil from the universe at the end of time -- and the rehabilitation of all evil-doers, including their return to grace, according to the ancient religion of Zoroastrianism. Zoroastrians believe that all of world history can be split up into four ages, each lasting 3,000 years. In the first age, the good god Ahura Mazda did his creating. In the second age, the Zoroastrian Lucifer, Ahriman, was born out of darkness, and he and his devilish minions started attacking Ahura Mazda's creation, including the human race, which stemmed from Gayomart, the primeval man who sired the first couple, Mashya and Mashyoi, the Zoroastrian Adam and Eve. In the third age, the prophet Zoroaster, founder of Zoroastrianism, appeared. Spiritual warfare heated up: Ahriman killed the primeval man Gayomart, and the leaderless Mashya and Mashyoi foolishly submitted to Ahriman's rule, for which they were damned to hell till the end times.

In the fourth and last age, the savior Saoshyant is to come to earth to purify the universe of evil. In those end times, called *Frashkart*, the souls of the dead will be reunited with their bodies in a general Resurrection. The earth will then be flooded with molten metal. Living humans and their dead ancestors will all be covered with this searing torrent, although to the righteous, this horrible lava will only feel like warm milk. In an Armageddon-type battle, the evil Ahriman will struggle in vain with the triumphing Ahura Mazda.

The Sassanid Zoroastrians believed that all evil beings in the universe would be cleansed at this time and restored to goodness and happiness.

**Fravashi**. In Zoroastrianism, the religion of the ancient and huge Persian Empire, this is the eternal part of an individual who acts as his guardian spirit while the person's soul is on earth. While a person's limited personality struggles on earth, the fravashi part of him lives continually in the light of heaven.

**Fylgir**. (The Followers) In the pagan Germanic religion, the fylgir acted like guardian spirits of individuals. Here's how the theory went: A person's mind might sometimes be seen outside his body, from a distance, taking the form of an animal which has the same traits as the person. For example, a brave warrior might spot a bear or an eagle; a sly schemer a fox; a merciless tyrant a wolf. This animal familiar spirit, or animal-like image of the person's soul, was called *fylgja*, the "follower" or the "companion." Acting like a guardian spirit, the fylgja (plural form, *fylgir*) went ahead of its owner in dangerous situations. Mostly, it stayed invisible and could only be seen in dreams or at the moment of death. The death of a fylgja was believed a sign of the coming death of its owner. (The fylgja could die because it is not the immortal part of a human.)

**Gabriel**. (Hero of God) The archangel Gabriel's main job is to be a messenger -- the announcer and news bearer of God's will -- heaven's town crier. Gabriel's most famous message was the news he brought to the Virgin Mary that the Palestinian peasant girl would be the mother of Christ, according to Bible legend. As for Moslems, they believe that the message-bearing Gabriel dictated the Koran to the prophet Mohammed. When a brilliantly white Gabriel confronted this former Arab merchant, he asked Allah's prophet-to-be: "Sleeper, how long will you sleep?" But it will be at the end of time when Gabriel's most earth-shattering announcement will come: He will blow the final trumpet. This blast will wake the sleeping dead, and they will prepare themselves for the Final Judgment. At that time, there will occur the separation of the sheep and the goats (righteous and sinners), the wheat and the tares -- according to traditional lore.

Besides practicing journalism, Gabriel also acts as heaven's treasurer. And he serves as heaven's chief ambassador to humanity. In fact, one legend claims that Gabriel instructs a newly incarnating soul, taken from heaven, for the nine months that it gestates in its mother's womb. As if all these duties are not enough, folklore also says Gabriel is an interpreter of dreams and visions. In one Old Testament legend, he helped the prophet Daniel figure out a puzzling end-of-the-world vision he had had, symbolized by the adventures of a ram and a goat. Some writers think Gabriel was the angel who fought in a tag-team match with the guardian angel of Persia for three weeks, eventually relieved by Michael. (A celestial roughhouse reported in the Old Testament Book of Daniel). Clement cites legends that have Gabriel foretelling the birth of Samson and the Virgin Mary, actions which caused Gabriel to be considered the angel of childbirth. Artists like to show Gabriel carrying a lily (Mary's flower), a scroll and a scepter.

In **Closer to the Light**, Melvin Morse cites a Jewish Talmudic legend in which Gabriel creates the Roman Empire to punish the Jews for something King Solomon had done in the 900s B.C. It seems the Hebrew king had allowed Pharaoh's daughter to teach him to play a thousand musical instruments, each one's melody to honor a different false god of Egypt. This occurred after their marriage. That same day, Gabriel retaliated by sticking a rod into the sea. Around the rod, an island gradually formed. On that island, the Empire of Rome was founded, the empire that eventually conquered Israel and scattered the Jews into exile all over the world.

In Milton's *Paradise Lost*, Gabriel commands a detachment of angels guarding (unsuccessfully) the still-sinless Adam and Eve in the Garden of Eden against any attempt by Satan to disrupt their lives. Satan, kicked out of Paradise after losing the War in Heaven, was known to be looking for revenge. The angels worried that God's new creation, Man, would be a likely target for Lucifer, so they beefed up security around Eden.

By some accounts, Gabriel is made of fire. And some Jewish sources credit him with causing the rain of fire and brimstone that destroyed Sodom and Gomorrah.

**Gehenna**. The Jewish purgatory and hell. Originally, ancient Jews believed that everybody, good and bad, went after death to a shadowy, joyless underworld called *Sheol* (See Sheol). Later, though, some Jews began to conceive of a heaven and hell, thinking that spiritually laggard Jews -- and Gentiles of all stripes -- went to the hellish place, called Gehenna (after the name of a Jerusalem area garbage dump where never-ending fires burned to consume the trash.) For the bad Jews, Gehenna was a temporary purgatory, but for Gentiles an everlasting hell.

**Gender of Angels**. Theologians have often considered angels to be *androgynous*: In other words, angels don't have a divided male or female sexuality. In this theory, each angel would combine maleness and femaleness within itself in a perfected wholeness, a unity that goes beyond the normal understanding of sexuality. Whether angels are androgyns or not, they often are perceived as either male or female by persons who feel they have a guardian angel. Nevertheless, it has been common for Christian artists to blur sexual distinctions when they portray angels -- frequently showing them as effeminate youths. Jesus himself was asked to address this issue, according to the New Testament. At the time, he was being confronted by "Sadducees" -- members of a Jewish sect that did not believe in life after death. The Sadducees asked him a hypothetical question about a widow who, in turn, married seven brothers as each of them died. Who was to be her husband in heaven, they asked. Jesus' response: "...when the dead rise to life, they will be like the angels in heaven and will not marry."

**Genius**. Today, the word means a mental giant. But in ancient times, a *genius* was the guardian spirit of a Roman male. A Roman woman's spirit was called a *Juno*. In fact, Roman birthday celebrations honored the genius, not the human.

And some scholars suspect that a growing belief in guardian spirits may have caused the custom of celebrating birthdays to become more and more popular in ancient times.

**Ghosts versus Angels**. Ghosts and angels are often confused in the popular mind. In the strictest sense, an angel is a superior heavenly being standing between man and God in the cosmic order. When an angel appears, it often displays a brilliant light and an enormous spiritual power. A ghost, on the other hand, is simply the spirit of a mortal who has died but, for some reason, is lingering on earth. The person experiencing the ghost is not in the presence of a superior being and does not feel the overwhelming spiritual power or see the brilliant light mentioned above. On the contrary, ghosts tend to look pale or washed-out. Sometimes, ghosts can take on a solid, 3-D appearance of their former selves. Angels always show up on a mission: to comfort a depressed person, for example. And sometimes a ghost does likewise. For example, the ghost's dalliance on earth may be because a departed loved one wants to continue looking after living relatives left behind. On the other hand, a ghost may be *earthbound*, as the parapsychologists say; that is, trapped on the earthly plane because of an addiction to physical existence. Or the lingering may result from the soul's being "shell-shocked" by a violent death; or a number of other undesirable reasons.

**Glory of Angels**. This expression refers to a large number of angels crowding around God, the Trinity or the Virgin Mary, as often portrayed by artists, for example. Some artists like to have the main worshipful figure surrounded by rings of descending angelic orders (from the high seraphim and cherubim on down the line). The inmost circle of high seraphim angels often glows red, a color symbolizing love; the next circle (for the cherubs) is blue, the emblem of light and knowledge; etc. By renaissance times, artists had begun ignoring this color system, according to Clara Clement in her *Angels in Art*.

**Golden Age of Man**. In Greek mythology, the gods created five types of human beings (in succession) and should have quit with the first batch, while they were still ahead. Experimenting with metals as building materials, the gods first created a Golden Race, which lived in total happiness, free of aging, hard work or sorrow. When this race died out, the spirits of these mortals stayed behind on earth to act as guardians over the inferior species which the Gods afterward created. The gods used other metals to make these lesser humans, such as silver and brass, and finally ended up using iron, thus creating the worst race of all, our present species.

**Guardian Angel**. This the lowest of nine orders of angels, each human getting one at birth, according to the Catholic Church's traditional belief. However, the Talmud, the famous ancient body of Jewish law and commentaries, notes that every Jew has 11,000 guardian angels. In our time, persons reporting on their guardian angels sometimes feel they have more than one, or even one or more angels who are relieved by another shift of guardians after a period of time.

**The Hebrew patriarch Jacob wrestles with an angel before dawn at Peniel. (Gustav Dore illustration)**

In the Gospel of Matthew, Jesus is quoted as saying that children have guardian angels: "See that you don't despise any of these little ones. Their angels in heaven, I tell you, are always in the presence of my father." The Roman Catholic Church's feast in honor of guardian angels is on Oct. 2.

**Guardian Spirit**. Frequently, when people talk about their "guardian angels," it becomes clear that they aren't referring to a classic religious angel -- a superior spiritual being, higher than mankind in the cosmic order. Rather, these people seem actually to be talking about what might better be called a "guardian spirit" -- typically a dead loved one who continues to look after them. A few such cases:

■ A teen-age boy was in a close football match. By chance, he looked out at the grandstand and saw his late grandfather smiling at him. The boy's widowed grandmother mentioned this to me later.

■ A sensible and intelligent widow told me she was once paralyzed with fear as a vehicle pulled into her path in traffic. As she skidded helplessly into what looked to be a severe crash -- her late husband, dead for several years, suddenly materialized in the car, seized the steering wheel and directed the car safely into a ditch. Then, he dematerialized. She was left shaken but unharmed, she said.

■ A heartbreaking and heart-warming story from Paul Swope of Lebanon, Oregon, as recounted in the January 1987 issue of *Fate*: One day, as a boy, Swope rushed into his house from school, waving a good report card. But he discovered his older sister Hazel standing at his parents' bedroom door looking scared. "Babe was in her playpen crying," Swope said in an account to Alice Swope. A doctor standing over Swope's unmoving mother snapped off his stethoscope and shook his head. "Hazel began to scream and Dad moaned. Babe continued to cry." After his mother's death, a deep depression set in for the 10-year-old Swope. "I'd sit in my mother's rocker, trying to remember every word of the stories she had read us." One night, Swope was in his bed sobbing when he suddenly felt a cool hand caressing his forehead. He slapped his hand to his head and for just a moment, he felt warm and soft fingers and love "radiating into my soul." Although now an adult with children of his own, Swope said he feels that somehow his mother is still close to him and watching over his entire family.

**Hadarniel**. (Greatness of God) The classic obstructionist gatekeeper. More than 60 myriads of parasangs tall (2.1 million miles or nine times the mean distance between the earth and the moon), the towering Hadarniel threatened Moses for coming up to heaven to get the Torah (the Bible's first five books containing the Law of Moses) from God. Hadarniel didn't realize that the Lawgiver had God's permission to get this all-important document for use on earth. When Moses started weeping from fear, God himself suddenly stepped into the fray, testily upbraiding Hadarniel: "You angels have been quarrelsome since the day I created you." For previously giving him a hard time over creating Adam, God reminded Hadarniel and the angels, "My wrath was kindled against you, and I burned scores of you with my little finger."

Hadarniel naturally underwent a quick change of attitude and agreed to act as Moses' humble guide. Having Hadarniel in his corner was a plus for Moses since, when this angel spoke the will of God, his voice reverberated through 200,000 heavens. Nevertheless, Moses still had to successfully debate the fire-breathing Angels of Terror surrounding the Throne of Glory, who tried to persuade God to keep the sacred Torah in heaven and not waste it on the mortal "dwellers of the dust," according to Ginzberg's *The Legends of the Jews*, Volume III.

**Hafaza**. In moslem legend, these are guardian angels who protect individuals against jinn and other evil spirits (See Jinn). Each person has a troop of four hafaza, two watching over him during the day and two at nighttime. This quartet continually writes down all the person's good and bad deeds. The most dangerous time for a mortal is at dawn or twilight, during the changing of the angelic guard, when the jinn try to take advantage of the situation. The logbooks of the hafaza scribes will be entered as evidence in the individual's case on Judgment Day.

**Halo**. Painters often stylize the halo as a thin, luminous ring over the head of a saint, angel or other religious figure. Or the halo might be shown as a solid golden disk behind the head. In either case, the halo is a symbol of virtue or innocence. So how did a ring of light around the head get associated with virtue? There is a common metaphysical theory that a prominent aura or bright light radiates from the head of a highly spiritual person.

This energy is part of a person's spirit body of light. The aura is normally invisible, but can supposedly be seen by psychics. Actually, the outline of this body of light is said to extend beyond the flesh -- not only beyond the head but also beyond the trunk, arms and legs. In German, the halo is simply called "holy shine." (The actual word "halo" comes from the Greek word for a threshing floor where oxen walked in a continual circular path.)

**Hardshells in Heaven**. In his book *Entertaining Angels*, Unitarian minister F. Forrester Church, son of the famous late Idaho Sen. Frank Church, has a chapter entitled *Heaven as Hell*, full of imaginary stories of what happens to fundamentalists arriving in a heaven radically different from what they expect. In one tale (which Church takes from C.E.S. Wood's satirical *Heavenly Discourse*), the famed fundamentalist preacher Billy Sunday arrives in heaven and is shocked to learn that God's favorite conversationalists are the brilliant atheist Voltaire, the religiously unorthodox American Revolution pamphleteer Thomas (*Common Sense*) Paine and the ancient Greek poetess Sappho. Meanwhile, other religious hardliners like Sunday are arriving in heaven, failing to recognize the place and leaving again. Sunday tells God that He needs a red-hot revival meeting to convert the heavenly heathen. The story ends with God suggesting that the meeting might better be held in the other afterlife realm.

**Harps and the Music of Heaven**. Angels playing harps or other musical instruments are a common scene in paintings -- an artist's symbol for the unearthly beautiful music reportedly heard in heaven, the so-called "music of the spheres." The noted parapsychologist D. Scott Rogo collected cases in which witnesses supposedly have heard such awesomely beautiful music while attending someone's death, cases in which the dying person himself or someone just brushing with death has heard the music, and other cases in which the music was just heard spontaneously. "The greatest music on earth, be it Brahms or Bach, is nothing but an inharmonious jangle of crude sounds by comparison. It was literally celestial..." Rogo quoted psychical researcher Raymond Bayless as saying of his own spontaneous encounter in Rogo's article *The Harmonies of Heaven* in the November 1988 issue of *Fate* magazine. Rogo noted the medieval British mystic Richard Rolle's belief, based on personal experience, that an inner music lies deep inside the soul and can be heard during a religious ecstasy. "According to some schools of yoga," Rogo added, "a life stream in the universe expresses itself through cosmic sounds which a person can hear during meditation. The music expressed within this life-stream is called *Nad* or *Nada*..." A survey in Britain of near-death experiences by Dr. Margot Grey in the mid-1980s turned up the fact that in 11 percent of 41 cases, this celestial music was heard, Rogo said.

**Harut and Marut**. Ancient Jews thought that only a few hundred angels fell, and did so because they fornicated with mortal women. Later, Christians decided that it was an entire third of the heavenly host that fell, and not because of lust but because of Satan's arrogance and rebellion. (And many Christians believed that the number of saved mortals would one day exactly equal the number of fallen angels, so that mankind could take their place in heaven.) But in Mohammedism, the number of fallen angels was reduced to only a handful of angels, including Iblis, the Moslem devil.

Here is the story of two such Moslem fallen angels, Harut and Marut: At the dawn of time, perhaps even in Adams' day, according to a family of legends, the angels talked scornfully to Allah about how sinful and rotten the mortals on earth had become. "You wouldn't have done any better if you had been in their place," Allah retorted. The angels didn't accept that and offered to send a winged delegation down to earth as an experiment to see if God was right. So the angels Harut and Marut went down as guinea pigs -- under strict orders to refrain from such grievous sins as worshipping idols, pursuing whores, committing murder or drinking wine. But, in most versions of the legend, they soon ran into a beautiful woman, made a pass at her, but found that she wouldn't yield unless they committed the very sins that Allah had forbidden. Finally, they agreed to drink wine, the least of the sins, but they got drunk. And then they murdered a passer-by who witnessed the imbibing. Meanwhile, the woman uttered the secret name of God, which she had gotten the hapless angels to blab, and this utterance magically lifted her up to heaven, still untouched, where she became a lovely star -- some say Venus.

As for luckless Harut and Marut, all their sinning disabled their wings, and they were no longer able to return to heaven at the end of each earthly day. The heavenly choirs had to admit that Allah was right.

**Hayy**. In legend, the always wandering angel who once tutored the medieval Persian Avicenna (one of the greatest Moslem philosophers) about the mysteries of the universe. One of those is that a human being is a hybrid of two natures -- a guardian angel, the side of the human spirit which still has a window on heaven, as well as a "fallen" soul.

**Hermes**. This angel-like Greek god wore winged sandals and a winged helmet. And he had some important jobs later considered the work of angels. Hermes (Mercury, to the Romans) brought messages, helped mortals, and led the souls of the newly dead into the afterlife. Eventually, some ancient Jewish writers rechristened Hermes as the angel *Hermesiel*.

**Holy Immortals**. A top-ranked group of six or seven archangels in the former world religion of the massive ancient Persian Empire, Zoroastrianism, nearly wiped out by the Moslem expansion of the 600s and today the faith of only about 250,000 persons in Iran and India. These archangel Holy Immortals are the attendants of the one God, Ahura Mazda, the "Wise Lord." They emanate (were born out of) this single God, and they are his personified traits. Opposed to the Holy Immortals were seven powerful arch-fiends, who became the forerunners of Christianity's seven deadly sins.

The Holy Immortals include Vohu Manah (Good Thought) -- who appeared to the prophet Zoroaster to help him start his religion; Asha Vahishra (Best Truth); Khshahra Vairya (Desirable Power); Spenta Armaiti (Benevolent Devotion); Haurvatat (Health); and Ameretat (Life). Best Truth, for example, symbolizes the universal order of things, while Desirable Power stands for the strength a human gets when he unites with and communes with the Divine Principle. In short, these archangels protect the most critical parts of the universe.

**Huris**. Black-eyed female angel-like beings in the Moslem Paradise who provide men with sexual pleasure, a striking departure from the Christian heaven, which lacks eroticism. On reaching Paradise, each Moslem man is assigned 72 huris, according to Moslem folklore. And every time sex is performed, each huris gets back her virginity afterward. The *huris* are somewhat like the Hindu *apsaras*. (See Apsaras)

**Iblis or Shaytan** (From the Greek word Diabolos, devil, and the Hebrew word Satan). The Moslem Satan. At first, Iblis was God's governor over the earth and the lower heavens, and also treasurer of Paradise. But according to the Koran, Iblis got into trouble for refusing to bow before Allah's newest creation -- Adam. Allah told the angels to prostrate themselves before the first man, and everybody did, except Iblis. "I'm better than he is," Iblis protested to Allah. "You made me (and the other angels) out of fire. You made him out of mud." Allah then damned Iblis for his arrogance.

Iblis got revenge, though, by talking Hawwa (Eve) into eating the forbidden fruit of the Tree of Evil, for which she was punished by Allah with menstruation, pregnancy, and the pain of childbirth. After Adam and Hawwa were thrown out of Paradise, they made a pilgrimage to Mecca.

But there is also a touching variant of the story of Iblis' damnation by Allah. As some Moslem Sufi mystics told it, Iblis was actually thinking positively, not negatively, when he refused to bow. Iblis' refusal was not because he thought he was better than Adam, but because he loved Allah the most out of all the angels, and he therefore wished to bow only before the Almighty. Also, Iblis was honoring Allah's earlier command not to pay homage to anyone but Him. However, Allah misunderstood Iblis' gesture as defiance, and the Almighty immediately banished Iblis forever from His divine presence -- a loss which was tantamount to hell. Nowadays, Iblis' only comfort throughout eternity is to hear the everlasting echo of his beloved Allah's harsh words condemning him to exile.

**Iniaes**. Originally a good angel, Iniaes was infuriated when he learned he was on a list of seven angels denounced by the Church in 745 A.D., and he found a unique way to take revenge. Defecting to the hellish side, Iniaes nowadays delights in breaking wind whenever an overly pompous preacher makes a deep remark, according to mythology cited by writer Malcolm Godwin. What started this myth? There actually was an historical angel-busting church council under Pope Zachary. The church council denounced a number of angels as false, including Raguel and Uriel, and the Church ordered that only the three angels mentioned in the Bible by name should henceforth be called on for help (i.e., Michael, Gabriel and Raphael). This crackdown was prompted by a population explosion of angels in the imaginations of common believers -- who had pretty much created a separate angel to preside over everything under the sun, from hailstones to the procurement of women. (See Suffix Angels)

**Intellect of Angels.** A common opinion of philosophers is that higher angels understand things with fewer, more far-reaching ideas than lower angels, who need many more less inclusive ideas to comprehend. In the same way, physicist Isaac Newton saw much more in the legendary falling apple than a chance to eat. But all angels, high or low, had their ideas implanted in their minds by God when they were created, and this keeps the angel's intellect free from error -- according to this theory. In other words, an angel's understanding of things is "built-in," -- made in heaven, so to speak -- and this knowledge doesn't come from thinking things out (with sometimes faulty reasoning), as humans would have to. Of course, although the above views have been popular, they are only speculation; one set of ideas among competing theories.

**Isa.** The Moslem name for Jesus. As the Moslems see it, Jesus is a semi-angel. Isa is among the heavenly beings who are closest to Allah's throne. On earth, Isa was a miracle-working prophet, healing, resurrecting the dead, even making clay birds, then breathing life into them. Isa escaped being crucified because his appearance was transferred to another who was executed in his place. God eventually took Isa, physical body and all, up to heaven.

**Israfil.** Israfil is the Islamic angel in charge of Judgment Day, who will blow the final trumpet on that climactic occasion while standing on the holy rock in Jerusalem. This trumpet blast will wake the sleeping dead from their graves. Currently, according to legend, this doomsday angel looks down into hell six times a day and is so stricken by grief over the grisly sight that Allah has to continually stop his gushing tears from flooding the earth. Israfil is also the Islamic angel of music and has the most beautiful face in creation. As he praises Allah in a thousand languages, Allah uses Israfil's breath to spawn hundreds of thousands of angels to join in the chorus of praise for the Almighty. Israfil is covered with hair, mouths and tongues. And he is colossal: Although his feet are under the seventh earth, his head is as high as the pillars of Allah's throne. His doomsday trumpet is an animal horn that is honeycombed on the inside, and in these interior cells of the horn, the souls of the dead slumber until Judgment Day.

**Ithuriel.** In Milton's *Paradise Lost*, Gabriel learns that Satan is loose in the Garden of Eden and could pose a danger to the sinless Adam and Eve. So he sends angels out to search for the arch-fiend. Finally, two angels, Ithuriel and Xaphan, find Satan. He is disguised as a toad, squatting at the ear of a sleeping Eve, whispering temptation. This is causing Eve to have a foul dream. When Ithuriel touches Satan with his spear, the metal causes him to resume his true form.

Satan is so ugly he is unrecognizable. For the moment, the hellish villain is foiled, but his whispered words have already planted the evil seed in Eve's mind.

**Jacob's Ladder**. This is the staircase leading from earth to heaven that the ancient Jewish patriarch Jacob saw in a dream at a holy place, according to a legend in the Bible's Book of Genesis. In the dream, Jacob saw angels going up and down the staircase, and then he noticed God standing beside him. God promised to give Jacob and the Jews descending from him the land Jacob was lying on, and the Lord promised that the Jewish race would be as numerous as "the specks of dust on the earth." Jacob woke up afraid, said to himself: "What a terrifying place this is. It must be the house of God; it must be the gate that opens into heaven." So Jacob named the placed *Beth-el*, Hebrew for "House of God."

**Jaoel**. In Jewish lore, the great angel Jaoel is the heavenly choir director who once escorted the Jewish patriarch Abraham on a visit Abraham made to heaven -- not suspecting that he was going to ask hard and perhaps embarrassing questions of God. The trip began as the father of the Jewish race flew on the back of a pigeon up to heaven. When the patriarch got in front of the divine throne, he repeatedly asked head-scratching questions -- to which he got no clear answer, even from all-knowing God. Why, Abraham asked God, did the Almighty give evil such terrible power to do all the harm that it does in His creation? And furthermore, Abraham asked, why did God allow man to have the will to do any evil in the first place?

No answers were forthcoming, but God did allow the patriarch a vision of all the earth's future -- no small feat but still a lot easier than tackling the philosophical problem of evil. In his 1952 book *Fallen Angels*, scholar Bernard J. Bamberger summarized this story, which appears in the Jewish *Apocalypse of Abraham*.

**Jinn**. In Arabian folklore, this is a race of good and evil invisible spirits, who once were on a par with the angels. But when their chief, Iblis (See Iblis) refused to worship the newly created Adam, Iblis and his jinn subordinates were demoted and exiled from Paradise. Iblis became the Moslem devil. Many of the jinn became troublesome tricksters, harassing mortals. But some of them became friendly to humans, helped mankind, and in some cases converted to Islam. In the *Arabian Nights*, for example, a good jinni (genie) helped Alladin when he rubbed his magic lamp. The jinns are made out of fire and lived on earth before mankind was created.

**Joel**. In the mythological *Book of Adam and Eve*, the angel Joel told Adam to name all the things and creatures in the world.

**Jonathan Smith**. The modern TV angel who attracted a weekly prime-time audience of millions. The former *Bonanza* and *Little House* star the late Michael Landon played this human-like angel on the show *Highway to Heaven*. Although Smith has supernatural powers, he prefers to coax human beings into solving their own problems by helping each other.

In a 3,000-year period, Cherubs have gone through a stunning evolution from monstrous guardians of places to cute, winged babies.

**Jophiel**. ("The Beauty of God") By some accounts, Jophiel guarded the Tree of Knowledge in Eden, drove Adam and Eve out of the Garden of Eden, and watched over Noah's three sons. His symbol is a flaming sword.

**Ka**. In ancient Eygptian belief, this is an exact replica of the physical body, made up of finer, subtler matter. It guards the soul and acts as its companion both during this life and the after-life. In some ways, the ka's essence is like the modern idea of an *astral body*.

**Kakabel**. In folklore, Kakabel is a powerful angel in charge of the stars and the star groupings of the sky. Some ancient writers consider him righteous and exalted. But to others, he is one of the evil angels who fell by mating with mortal women and then compounded the error by teaching mortals astrology and the constellations.

**Kemuel**. ("The congregation of God") A gatekeeper of heaven, Kemuel once tried to keep Moses from passing when he ascended to heaven at God's bidding to get the Torah and bring it back to Mount Sinai and to the wilderness-wandering Jews. For his presumption, Kemuel was struck by Moses who "destroyed him out of this world." This must have been a fearsome blow. It apparently discouraged any thought of retaliation by the head gatekeeper's staff of 12,000 fiery angels of destruction, all posted there with Kemuel at the portals of the sky -- presumably to dishearten any would-be trespassers. The full account is in Ginzberg's *The Legend of the Jews*, Volume III.

**Lahash**. Once, when Moses prayed to God concerning death, the wrong-headed angels Lahash and Zakun teamed up to intercept the prayer before it reached the divine ear. This apparently was so monumental a task, that they were helped by 184 myriads of spirits (1.84 million, or just under the population of West Virginia). Lahash and co-conspirator Zakun were whipped with 60 fiery lashes as punishment, according Jewish legend.

**Lailah**. The legendary Jewish Angel of Night, in charge of conception. When a woman conceives, Lailah carries the sperm before God, who decides what kind of human being will come from it -- rich or poor, male or female, beautiful or ugly, etc. God then summons a pre-existing soul to be thrust into the woman's embryo. The soul protests about being forced to leave the pleasant spiritual world, but to no avail. The soul is railroaded into the woman's womb by an angelic guard who makes sure it does not try to escape. An angel gives the soul a preview of its coming earthly existence, but just before birth, the angel fillips the baby's nose, and the child forgets its knowledge of the future.

**Lares**. In ancient Rome, these were the protective household godlings who were offered food at every meal. The head *Lar* was the spirit of the family's founder.

**Lifespan of Angels**. Most authorities say angels will live forever -- like the human soul, both being made of indestructible spirit.

Indeed, Christian artists have often showed angels as youths to symbolize their immortality. Although believers generally agree that angels will never die, that does not mean they are eternal. Only God always existed. Angels came later as part of God's creation of the universe, and, some claim, before any other creature.

**Lilith**. A demonness, Lilith was Adam's first wife before Eve, in Jewish legend. Adam had gotten jealous when he noticed that all the other animals had mates. So God made Lilith for him -- but out of filth and sediment, not the dust He used to make Adam. All sorts of marital problems developed. During sex, Lilith was not satisfied to merely lie under Adam but wanted other positions -- because, she said, she was Adam's equal. After the relationship failed to work out, she eventually became one of several women bedded by Lucifer. As the first wife of Adam, Lilith showed herself to be a wild, wanton and monstrous woman, fornicating with demons to produce scores of offspring daily. Lilith's attractive daughters, the so-called *Lilim*, enjoy seducing sleeping celibate monks by appearing in their dreams to get them sexually involved. After Adam's and Lilith's marital fiasco, God created Eve.

**Limbo**. In Roman Catholic theology, this is the place where the noble pagans of antiquity went after they died -- the virtuous ancient heathens who lived before Christ was born to save mankind from hell. After his resurrection, Christ brought these pagans to heaven. Meanwhile, unbaptized infants and others free of personal sin also find their way to Limbo.

In Limbo, a soul enjoys a natural happiness, but not the supernatural bliss that comes with being in heaven, so the thinking goes. Limbo was an attempt by the Church to better explain God's justice. It provided a way for the "innocent" who didn't have an opportunity to follow God's plan of salvation to escape punishment. The term Limbo comes from the Latin word *limbus* meaning border -- a reflection of the ancient belief that this realm is located on the periphery of hell. Despite speculations by theologians, the Catholic Church hierarchy has no official position on the topic.

**Malaika** (messengers). The Moslem name for angels. In the Moslem universe, by some accounts, the angels keep a record book of each person's good and bad deeds. On Judgment Day, these books will be handed out. The righteous will have their record books placed in their right hands, and they will go up to heaven. The wicked will receive their books in their left hands and go down to hell. In Paradise, beautiful angel-like women called *huris* will wait on the men and give them sexual pleasure. The Moslem angels, made out of light, also stand guard at the edge of heaven to keep the evil jinns and other demons, all made out of fire, from eavesdropping.

**Malik**. In the Koran, the righteous angel Malik is the overseer of hell, not Iblis (Lucifer). The tortured ones in hell, handled by 19 angel guards called "violent thrusters," cry out to their keeper: "Oh, Malik!" The hard-nosed Malik stirs up the fires that sear these agonized souls and answers their complaints by cracking jokes.

Nevertheless, the tortured can at least escape the violent thrusters by reciting the religious formula: "Allah, the Compassionate, the Merciful." Actually, the Muslim sinners in hell get more sensitivity from Malik than do the roasting infidels. After all, Malik knows that the true believers, even those who have committed mortal sins, will one day be freed from hell by Mohammed's intervention.

**Mammon.** A fallen angel in Middle Ages folklore whose name is now a generic term for greed, a lust for worldly riches. In English, the term "mammon" has become a personification of money as a false god for the greedy. In Puritan John Milton's poem *Paradise Lost*, the angel Mammon, before he fell during the War in Heaven, was in the habit of looking down at heaven's golden pavement rather than up at God. As a result, he was stooped over in stature. After the fall, it is money-minded Mammon who finds the underground precious metal (in a volcano) which the devils use to build their hellish capital city, Pandemonium. Later, this prince of greed became hell's ambassador to England, according to the claim of some Continental occultists who were perhaps upset by British commerce. The term "mammon" goes back to Jesus' comments in the Gospels: "No man can be a slave to two masters; he will hate one and love the other; he will be loyal to one and despise the other. You cannot serve both God and mammon (greed for worldly riches)."

**Man Clothed in Linen**. In the Old Testament, the prophet Ezekial has a vision of a future time when a furious Yahweh decides to mercilessly punish wicked Israel for disobeying him and worshipping idols. In his dream, the prophet sees Yahweh shouting for six armed angels to get ready for the terrible job, including one angel, "a man clothed in linen with a writer's inkhorn by his side." Yahweh sends this heavenly scribe ahead of the rest of the angelic troop with a special task: The linen-clad scribe is supposed to mark the foreheads of the righteous Jews who are disgusted by the wrongdoing that has been going on around them in the Israelite capital of Jerusalem. Ezekial describes what happens next: "And I heard God say to the other (angels following the scribe angel): 'Kill the old men, young men, young women, mothers and children. But don't touch anyone who has the mark on his forehead.'" Then, the brutal slaughter began, starting at the Temple, where religious leaders were slain. Actually, this vision was one of a number that Ezekial had. Some scholars think Ezekial's prophecies of doom took place a few years before the Babylonian King Nebuchadnezzer sacked Jerusalem and razed the Temple to punish the Jews for revolting against him. At that time, Jewish nobles were taken back to Babylon as hostages to guard against future insurrections. It was the beginning of the so-called "Babylonian Captivity" of the 500s B.C.

**Manna**. In folklore, this is the food of the angels and also of the righteous living in heaven. During their escape from slavery in Pharaoh's Egypt, the desert-wandering Israelites ate this mysterious food, which rained down on them from heaven, according to Bible legend. The strange food got the name "manna" -- Aramaic for "What is this?" -- because that's what the Hebrews asked when they saw it. The Bible describes manna as a thin, flaky substance that covered the ground and was "delicate as frost." The Bible continues: "It was like a small white seed and tasted like thin cakes made of honey. In fact, Bible scholars say there is indeed a nourishing substance similar to this Bible description on low tamarisk shrubs in the Sinai wilderness and other deserts. According to one study, this "manna" is excreted by plant lice and hardens in the dry desert air.

**Mara**. The Buddhist devil, who tried to sidetrack the Buddha's spiritual growth in a way similar to how Satan tried unsuccessfully to tempt Jesus to make himself the rich ruler of the earth. Mara's goal: To try to tempt the Buddha in order to upset his concentration while he meditated and therefore keep him from gaining enlightenment -- the necessary step to escaping the wheel of reincarnation and entering nirvana, the sublime state of cosmic consciousness. While the Buddha meditated for five weeks under a fig tree called the Tree of Wisdom, Mara first sent his three gorgeous dancing daughters to try to seduce him. Having failed to arouse lust, Mara next tried scare tactics, dispatching a pack of grotesque armed demons. Finally, in desperation, he threw a flaming discus at the serene meditator's head -- likewise unsuccessful. Although the Buddha became enlightened and finally understood the cause of suffering, he heeded the creator god Brahma's pleas and stayed on earth for a while to teach, rather than immediately rising to nirvana, never to be reborn again.

**Mary**. The mother of Christ is a human, not an angel, but Catholics revere her as the "Queen of the Angels," reigning over the celestial choirs. For centuries, Christian legend has had Mary comforting persons in utter despair, healing the sick, lessening the suffering of sinners in Purgatory (the halfway house between heaven and hell), and even sometimes robbing hell of some souls damned for mortal sins. In one medieval myth, the Devil, apparently frustrated by Mary's helpful deeds, says: "I complain daily to God of these injustices. But He is deaf where His Mother is concerned and leaves her lady and mistress of Paradise."

Originally, Christian artists showed Mary as relatively low in status, inferior even to the Three Wise Men, who had halos while she did not. But Mary filled the great need for a Mother symbol in ancient and medieval Christianity. By the 500s A.D., artists began granting her a halo, and by the 800s A.D., she was promoted to "Queen of the Angels." A few centuries later, during the high Middle Ages, her growing popularity eventually exceeded even Jesus'. In fact, the huge Gothic cathedrals were actually built for her. The belief even grew up that she had been taken up into heaven while alive -- never experiencing the normal death of a mortal.

Scores of supernatural appearances of Mary have been reported over the centuries. One of the most famous began in 1858 outside a French town called Lourdes in the foothills of the Pyrenees Mountains. On Feb. 11, 14-year-old shepherdess Bernadette Soubirous, whose peasant family was so poor it lived in an ex-jail cell, came upon a spiritual being in the form of a beautiful, white-robed teen-age girl.

By early next month, 20,000 people were on hand for the 15th appearance of the spirit, who eventually revealed herself as the Virgin Mary. The rocky cave area became a shrine, famous for its healing water, which draws three million visitors a year, a half million of them looking for a cure. By the mid-1970s, thousands of cures had been claimed, including 63 authenticated by the Catholic Church's thorough verification system.

Some believe Mary is literally appearing, others consider the visions to be archetypal images created out of the collective unconscious mind of humanity, and still others, of course, consider it fantasy. Whatever the case, the visions have profoundly affected the lives of thousands. On the home front, Mary has lent her name to Los Angeles. In the 1700s, the Spanish founders of the city dubbed it: "Nuestra Senora, la Reina de *los Angeles*" (Our Lady, the Queen of the Angels).

**Mastema**. (Enmity) In the mythical *Book of Jubilees*, Mastema is the "Father of Evil." He controls an army of evil spirits that plague the earth and are responsible for many of mankind's woes -- but Mastema is actually working for God as an official tempter, testing people's faith. The evil spirits under Mastema's leadership were born out of the dead bodies of a race of monstrous giants who were killed by God. (The giants themselves had been begotten by fallen angels mating with mortal women.) After the Flood, God tentatively granted Noah's prayer to imprison all the evil spirits underground. But at the last minute, Mastema successfully persuaded God to leave him at least a few troublemakers, because wicked mankind needed the continued chastening. By the way, this tale of giants with fallen angels for fathers -- and similar stories -- were uninhibited elaborations of a vague reference in the Bible's first book, Genesis: "...Some of the super-natural beings saw that these girls (on earth) were beautiful, so they took the ones they liked... In those days, and even later, there were giants on the earth who were the descendants of human women and the supernatural beings."

**Mefathiel**. (The Opener of Doors) Jewish folklore's guardian angel of thieves.

**Mehiel**. An angel who watches over writers, teachers and their ilk, according to Jewish kabbalist mystics.

**Mephistopheles**. (The Hater of the Light) This fallen archangel is a smooth talker and a master of etiquette, according to author Malcolm Godwin's synthesis of the medieval mythology. In some stories, Mephis-topheles is an agent of Lucifer, and in others he is the devil himself under another name -- such as in the various Faust legends about a man who sold his soul to the devil. In the most famous version of this story, Goethe's poetic play *Faust*, Heinrich Faust, a depressed scholar of enormous intellect, signs a con-tract in blood with Mephistopheles. Faust offers his soul for just a single moment of true satisfaction that he would want to stay with him for a while. With Mephistopheles' help, Faust becomes a powerful bureaucrat with the Holy Roman Empire, but he gluts the kingdom with worthless paper money. Also, Faust gets Helen of Troy, the most beautiful woman of the ancient world, as a lover, among other things. But Mephistopheles is ultimately foiled. For one thing,

But Mephistopheles is ultimately foiled. For one thing, Faust tires of a life of sensual abandon. And at the same time, Faust manages eventually to become a useful, not harmful official for the Empire. Faust's Texas-sized ego dissolves into service for others. Mephistopheles loses not just the soul of the born-again Faust but also a bet with God over whether Faust's soul could be tempted into damnation. (In Faust's play, Mephistopheles is just another name for Lucifer himself, although in other stories like this, Mephistopheles is a different devil.)

**Merkabah Rider.** An ancient or medieval Jewish mystic who fasted or repeatedly uttered prayers to get himself into an ecstatic trance. Then, like a shaman, he dispatched his soul upward through seven heavenly halls, trying to reach the high celestial world that contains God's Throne of Glory and the Chariot (*merkivah*) that supports it. Once there, the merkabah rider would try to penetrate the veil surrounding the Throne to get a firsthand look at the seat of power. If he could pass the hurtles and make it to the finishing line, so to speak, the rider would so elevate himself that he would join his soul with the Universal Soul. Along this hard journey, there were demons harassing the soul, but angels could help the journeyer. Therefore, before he started his mystic quest, the merkabah rider would pray, prepare magical talismans, utter incantations, and sometimes practice asceticism in the belief that all this would protect him.

**Metatron**. (The name's meaning is unclear, but "Closest to the Throne" is one possibility.) Sitting beside God, Metatron, the throne angel with 72 names, records Israel's good and bad deeds, and is one of the tallest angels in heaven.

In mystical Jewish lore, Metatron is one of heaven's greatest angels, and, by some accounts, he and the cherubim and seraphim are the only created beings allowed in God's throne room. One mystic said Metatron carries Jewish prayers up through 900 heavens to God. In certain folklore, it is Metatron who sustains the physical world.

According to one family of legends, Metatron was originally the upright mortal Enoch mentioned in the Book of Genesis who "walked with God." Enoch was so righteous as a human that God took him straight to heaven and transformed him into the angel Metatron with 365,000 fiery eyes -- turning his flesh into flames, his intestines into fire, and his bones into embers. In the mythical *Book of Enoch*, before being changed into Metatron, Enoch toured heaven, seeing the winds that blow the sun across the sky, the mountainous caves of Sheol where mortal ghosts wait for Judgment Day, and the confinement place of the fallen angels awaiting final damnation. The imprisoned angels asked the touring scribe to draw up a petition (ultimately unsuccessful) asking God for mercy. In heaven, Enoch was eventually changed into an angel of fire with innumerable eyes and three dozen wings.

Before this transformation, Enoch had been the greatest of mortal scribes. As Metatron, this work went on, since Metatron became heaven's secretary, recording the minutes of all the celestial and earthly doings for God's archives -- including logging down

Israel's good and bad deeds. On one occasion, the archangel Uretil told all the universe's secrets to Enoch, who took dictation round-the-clock for 30 days, filling some 360 volumes.

**Michael**. ("Who is like God?") Michael is the first and most powerful of God's created beings, God's chief soldier, and the most important angel. (In 1950, this "marshal of Paradise" was designated by Pope Pius XII as the patron angel of police officers.) In legend, Michael is a strong defender of righteousness. It was Michael who threw rebellious Satan out of heaven after he was defeated during the War in Heaven between the good and bad angels. This was appropriate, since Michael is the commander of the heavenly armies, even though he is traditionally considered only an archangel, the second lowest of the nine ranks of angels. Michael is also the guardian angel of righteous Israel and was the only national guardian angel not to be corrupted by his client country. (See *Ethnarchs*).

Michael is also the angel which legend puts in charge of conducting the souls of the newly dead into the afterlife. (In fact, commentators have mentioned that the old black spiritual, "Michael, row the boat ashore" seems to refer to the idea of Michael's helping the soul to cross the waters to the "other side.") Moreover, Michael is the angel of the Last Judgment, where he weighs the souls to determine their fate. Artists like to show him holding a pair of soul-weighing scales in his hand. According to Christian legends, Michael received the soul of the dying Madonna and guarded it until it could be reunited with her sinless body in heaven.

In his role as a defender of righteousness, Michael is traditionally believed to have a special power to purify evil places. During the Middle Ages, when she was tried by the English as a witch, Joan of Arc claimed that it was Michael, among other supernatural personalities, who emboldened her to drive the English out of France during the Hundred Years' War. In the Roman Catholic Church, the feast day of Michael, Raphael and Gabriel is on Sept. 29.

In *The Book of Adam and Eve* mythology, Michael, at God's command, brings the newly created Adam to the angels and tells them to fall down before the first man in respectful homage. Michael set an example by being the first to do so. But Satan balked, saying the it should be the other way around, since a human being was inferior to an angel and was created after the angels. God reacted by throwing Satan and his followers out of Paradise. The grieving, exiled angels were particularly upset to see how happy Adam was, the one they blamed for their catastrophe. Satan got revenge by tempting Eve while two angel guards at the Garden of Eden were temporarily away on a trip to heaven. After Satan's temptation caused Adam to be thrown out of Eden, a despondent Adam thought of murdering Eve in his anger. But he feared another divine penalty and besides, he was moved by Eve's sorrow. Michael came by and taught Adam how to farm so he could support his wife and newborn child, Cain. On another occasion, Michael swooped down in a fiery chariot and ferried Adam to heaven to see the burning face of God, who told him he would one day let him serve the Almighty again because he had shown a love for knowledge.

After Adam returned to earth, Michael used a rod to freeze the watery fluid surrounding heaven to make it impassable for trespassers. On his deathbed, surrounded by 63 children, Adam is pitied by God. The Almighty lifts his curse and turns the first man's soul over to Michael for cleansing in the Acherusian Stream.

**Michaelmas**. A term used by the English for the former feast of St. Michael the Archangel on Sept. 29. (See Angel Holidays)

**Mikal**. To the Moslems, this is the archangel Michael (See Michael). Mikal is humorless. He has never laughed since the time when hell was created. Created 5,000 years after the doomsday angel Israfil, Mikal lives in the Seventh Heaven, sporting emerald wings and a coat of saffron hairs. Each hair has a million faces, and on each face there are a million eyes and a million tongues, each tongue speaking a million languages, all of them begging Allah for forgiveness. Meanwhile, each eye is shedding 70,000 tears.

**Milton, John**. This blind Puritan poet wrote the greatest adventure poem in the English language, the angel-clogged 12-volume *Paradise Lost*. Milton's encyclopedic story has good versus bad angels throwing mountains around as they fight in heaven. Kicked out of the sky, the bad angels fall for days to hell, where they build a demon capital city, Pandemonium. But Satan takes revenge by corrupting Adam and Eve. During the 1600s, this blind poet -- who once visited Galileo when the church had the scientist imprisoned for saying the earth goes round the sun, not vice versa

-- dictated his angel-crowded masterpiece to various secretaries late in life. Milton followed the habit of ancient and medieval Christians of turning foreign gods into devils. In Paradise Lost, for example, Satan's rebel angels included Thammuz, a borrowing of the old Babylonian god Tammuz, who yearly died and was resurrected and remarried to his wife and sister, Ishtar, the goddess of love (a symbol of the annual farming cycle of growth and death).

**Minos.** Hell's judge in Dante's *Divine Comedy*. His job was to assign each newly arriving doomed soul to its particular place of torment. See *Dante*.

**Mithra.** (Friend) This 10,000-eyed angel in the ancient Persian religion of Zoroastrianism has an interesting birthday -- December 25 -- and it's no coincidence that it coincides with Christmas. In fact, ancient Christians took over Mithra's birthday to celebrate the birth of Jesus, since nobody really had a clear idea when Jesus was born. Here's how it came about:

In the religion of Zoroastrianism, from which Judaism and later Christianity got its ideas of heaven and hell and of warfare between good and bad angels -- Mithra was the head of the good spirits or *yazatas*. Mithra was the "right-hand man" of the good God, Ahura Mazda (the Pure Light) in his cosmic war with the evil spirit, Ahriman -- the Zoroastrian forerunner of Satan. Mithra's job was to keep the world from falling apart.

Later, by the time of the Roman Empire, Mithra had changed from an angel into a sun god, Mithras, and he now had his own religion -- Mithraism.

Roman soldiers and sailors -- depending on him to grant them life after death -- spread his worship quickly through the early Roman Empire. In fact, Mithra's religion soon became a big rival to young and growing Christianity. Indeed, Mithraism had a lot in common with Christianity, stressing humbleness, brotherly love, communion, baptism, life after death, Judgment Day, and the resurrection. One big difference, though, was that Mithraism tolerated other gods. But it was the similarities that were its undoing, as millions of Mithraites easily converted en masse to Christianity during the later years of the Roman Empire. Mithras' birthday, on Dec. 25, was a big pagan winter solstice festival for his worshipers (celebrating the fact that the sun had sunk as low in the winter sky as it was going to go and would now move higher again, lengthening the days). So for convenience, Christians pegged Mithras' birthday as an arbitrary time to celebrate Christ's birth, so Christians could have their own celebrations while the heathens partied.

**Moakibat**. (See Hafaza)

**Moroni**. The angel who, according to Mormon church founder Joseph Smith, visited him in 1823 at Palmyra, New York. Moroni allegedly told the 17-year-old Smith where to dig up golden plates studded with Egyptian-style hieroglyphics that Smith was said to have translated into the *Book of Mormon*. According to the *Book of Mormon*, ancient America was settled by a colony of refugees from the Tower of Babel. Smith eventually took about 50 wives before being shot to death by a mob in Carthage, Ill., in 1844.

**Dante and Beatrice reach Saturn during their climb through the heavens. (Gustav Dore illustration)**

**Movie Angels**. Hollywood has long been intrigued by the idea of angels interacting with human beings. Movie plots range from the classic 1946 Christmas-season film *It's a Wonderful Life*, where the angel Clarence showed hero George Bailey (Jimmy Stewart) what a unhappy world it would have been if he had never been born (See the entry "Clarence Oddbody"); to the 1990 blockbuster *Ghost*, that year's top-grossing film about a murdered newlywed husband (Patrick Swayze) who lingers on earth in spirit form to protect his beloved widow (Demi Moore) from the treacherous "best friend" who did him in.

Which brings up a point: As the two films show, some of Hollywood's celluloid angels are indeed bonafide angels from heaven while other "angels" are actually just plain folks who died and have unfinished business on earth or various adventures in the after-life.

Other angelic movies include: *The Bishop's Wife* (1947), with David Niven as a bishop who is visited by an angel (Cary Grant); *Forever Darling* (1956), where a feuding couple (Desi Arnez and Lucille Ball) are brought back together by a guardian angel (James Mason); *The Horn Blows at Midnight* (1945), a comedy and fantasy about an angel (Jack Benny) who is ordered to wipe out the earth by blowing a Doomsday trumpet a la Gabriel; *Here Comes Mr. Jordan* (1941), the classic tale of a boxer who dies prematurely and is therefore sent back to earth in the body of another person -- remade in 1978 as *Heaven Can Wait*, with the hero (Warren Beatty) playing football rather than taking swings and jabbing; Another movie also titled *Heaven Can Wait* (1943) but unrelated to the previous two films. This one is a comedy about a man (Don Ameche) who reflects upon his sinful life on earth while trying to get permission to enter heaven.

**Mulciber**. In Puritan poet John Milton's *Paradise Lost*, Mulciber was the fallen angel architect who designed Satan's capital city in hell -- Pandemonium ("All-Demons").

**Munkar and Nakir**. In some Moslem tradition, these two angels wake up the dead who are sleeping in their tombs, awaiting Resurrection Day and the Final Judgment to come at the end of the world. On the night after corpses are buried, Munkar and Nakir set the newly dead mortals upright. And without giving them time to prepare, they quiz them about their opinion of Mohammed. The believers will have the right answer -- that Mohammed is Allah's messenger. They will then be left in peace until Resurrection Day. But the infidels and sinners will be caught off-guard by this pop quiz. When the unbelievers fail to give a satisfactory answer, according to some authorities, the infidels will be continually beaten by Munkar and Nakir until Resurrection Day -- except on Friday, the Muslim sabbath. (Other authorities just say the wrongdoers will suffer a preliminary hell of sorts in their graves, even before their official damnation on Resurrection Day.)

**Nasargiel**. The upright angel who led Moses on a tour of hell. There, the Lawgiver saw a veritable "clothesline" of tortures -- men hanging by their eyelids for having looked lustfully at neighbors' wives on earth; others hanging by their ears for listening to blowhards' hot air and silly talk rather than recitations of the Torah; and so on. For his convenience, the hellfire withdrew from Moses for a distance of 500 parasangs (1,750 miles) while he was looking around, according to Volume II of Ginzberg's *The Legends of the Jews.*

**Near-Death Experience.** This is a term coined by physician Raymond Moody in the mid-1970s to describe the mystical experiences people sometimes have when they nearly die or face a life-threatening situation.

In a full-blown NDE, a person typically reports leaving the body, journeying through a dark "tunnel," emerging in a world of light, and being greeted by loved ones who preceded him in death, a religious figure, or a "being of light." The description of the being of light is usually consistent: a radiant, superior entity, a shapeless glow with a lively personality that is overwhelmingly loving and often concerned with helping the dying person evaluate his life on earth from a spiritual perspective. To that end, the dying mortal may view a three-dimensional, panoramic flashback of every tiny action in his life -- trying to determine to what extent he had learned to develop within himself a spiritual love.

How the individual identifies the being of light is a matter of his cultural background. Some might speak of seeing Jesus, some have called the being an angel or God himself, some feel it is the higher self. But whatever labels are used, the NDEers appear to be describing the same entity.

The NDE frequently ends when the person is told that it is not yet his time to die, or the near-death experiencer may selflessly ask to go back to care for someone left behind on earth. Pollsters estimate that eight to nine million Americans have had near-death experiences.

The near-death experience burst onto the mass consciousness in the mid-1970s with the publication of physician Moody's landmark *Life After Life*, which summarized Moody's informal collection of NDE experiences over several years. *Life After Life* touched off a number of scientific studies of the NDE. A generation after Moody's book appeared, interest still had not faded.

In March 1992, *Life* magazine did an NDE report, containing this typical story: Around 1980, Philadelphia nurse Grace Bulbuka arrived at a hospital with childbirth complications. As she passed out, she heard a voice shouting about her lack of blood pressure. Instantly, she was out of her body, looking down, watching frantic doctors and nurses rushing around, one of them, particularly upset, cursing. Next, Bulbuka was in a grey tunnel, feeling wind brushing her side. "I began to feel the most incredible, warm, golden, loving feeling, and the feeling was also a wonderful, warm, golden light." She found herself within this light. The light contained a presence, "a wisdom, and that wisdom was the final word. The wisdom loved me, and at the same time it knew everything about me." Bulbuka saw everything she had ever done on earth and every feeling associated with it. She wanted to move into the magnificent light and stay with it forever, but: "I was shown that I had to go back and take care of my two children."

**Neglect by Angels**. A frequently heard question concerning angels is: Why is one person saved by an angel but another allowed to suffer disaster. Why was Peter rescued by an angel from King Herod's prison in the Bible's Book of Acts while, in the same book, his fellow disciple, James, was executed by the sword? This is deep philosophy, and over the centuries, several theories have unfolded, none entirely satisfactory:

■ Some persons seem to be "wired" to interface better with the spiritual world. Such a sensitive person may receive a message while another might be oblivious to it, although the other side presumably was trying to "get through" in both instances.

■ Adversity is a teacher of spiritual lessons. Some learn honesty by being cheated or by suffering the consequences of cheating others.

■ One controversial and mystical theory is that misfortune suffered in this life may be the consequence of something in a "past life."

■ Karma, as the eastern religions call it, is also sometimes offered as an explanation for why bad things happen. The great American philosopher Ralph Waldo Emerson refers to it as the Law of Compensation -- the idea that the universe is a big echo chamber in which the good we do boomerangs back to us, sooner or later in one form or another -- and likewise the evil. An old timer might say, "What goes around, comes around." Or, to give a new twist to one of Newton's three laws of motion: "For every action, there is an equal and opposite reaction."

■ Still others say one can attract trouble to oneself by negative thinking, like hate or worry, until the subconscious mind eventually -- almost supernaturally -- turns a person's fixated thoughts into reality.

Regardless of which, if any, theory is correct, there simply is no clear, all-satisfying answer to why the angels "go on a holiday," as some have expressed this dilemma.

**Nergal**. The head of hell's secret police, according to Johann Weyer's *Pseudo Monarchia Daemonium*. The book purported to list all of hell's bureaucracy, but author Malcolm Godwin says it was actually a veiled lampoon of despised church leaders. In Weyer's book, hell is organized like a mirror image of medieval society, with different kingdoms and various classes of devils, including nobles and commoners. And each European country, Weyer added, also had an infernal ambassador, such as Thamuz to Spain and Hutjin to Italy. Incidentally, Beelzebub (q.v.) was in charge in Weyer's pecking order, Satan having the status of a dethroned monarch.

**Nephilim**. ("The Famed Ones") The race of giants spawned by the illicit mating of fallen angels with beautiful mortal women. (See Semjaza) Different stories about these titanic offspring variously describe them as heros, giants, superhumans or monsters. In the mythical *Book of Enoch*, they are 11,250 feet tall, about a third the height of Mt. Everest. According to some myths, it was the Nephilim who built the brick and tar Tower of Babel on the plain of Babylonia -- to force their way into heaven by climbing the tower.

God stopped that plan by confusing the world's one language, Hebrew, into many tongues. The Almighty eventually wiped out the nephilim by sending the Flood. Actually, one giant, Og, managed to survive by huddling onto the roof of Noah's Ark. Somehow, the patriarch found the time to feed Og 1,000 oxen a day through a trap door.

**Nicknames of Angels**. A sampling: "Birds of God" (Dante); "Breaths of God" (Lactantius); "Sons of God" (the Bible); "Watchers" (Book of Enoch). "Morning Stars" (The Bible -- an allusion to the fact that they are celestial and were already in existence early on when the human race was created.) "Chariots of God" (The Bible)

**Nike**. This ancient Greek goddess of victory -- whose name is known today mostly as an athletic brand -- gave her looks to the cause of angelhood. During the time of the Roman Empire's first Christian emperor Constantine, many angels in art began to take on the winged look of this goddess. Before then, most artists showed angels as wingless youths (the youthfulness symbolizing their immortality). Adding wings, though, introduced another symbol: The wings stand for, among other things, the fact that these spiritual beings can flit around with the speed of thought.

**Nimrod**. The mighty hunter mentioned in the Bible and also the legendary ramrod behind the building of the Tower of Babel. Since some ancient Jewish legends say the Tower was built by the *nephilim* (the sons of bad angels who fell by mating with beautiful mortal women), this would make Nimrod a son of a fallen angel.

Nimrod became a great hunter because of a priceless gift from his doting father, the Bible patriarch Cush: Cush handed down to him the magic skins which God had given to the naked Adam and Eve to cover them after they were thrown out of the Garden of Eden. Whenever hunter Nimrod wore these skins, the woodland animals just collapsed at the sight of him, and no human could beat him in a fight. The powerful Nimrod became more and more evil. Eventually, he conquered the world and blasphemously proclaimed himself a god. Finally, Nimrod's wrongdoing climaxed when his ministers proposed building a huge tower in Babylonia to enable humans to storm and plunder heaven itself.

The growing Tower was soon so tall that it took a year to climb it. And so, if a person fell from the top, the evil builders hardly noticed, but if a brick fell, it would take a year to replace, and the workmen weeped. The slave-drivers allowed no break-time. Pregnant women had to keep making bricks while giving birth. The mortals were so close to heaven, they shot arrows into the clouds, and the shafts fell back to earth, dripping with angelic blood.

Finally, God and the 70 angels who surround his throne had reached their wit's end over this unholy spectacle. The celestial leadership dropped down to earth and confused the unified language of the builders (Hebrew) into many different tongues to end the project. Some builders, in frustration at being suddenly unable to communicate, started fighting each other. Others of them God turned into apes and phantoms.

While God and his 70 angels happened to be on the earth, they cast lots over which angel would get guardianship over which of the 70 nations. Michael got Israel. (See Ethnarchs).

The divine assembly also assigned various languages to each country -- reserving for Israel the Hebrew language, the divine speech which God had used when He created the world. The full story appears in Ginzberg's *The Legends of the Jews*, Volume 1. Some scholars have suggested that the Tower of Babel story was inspired by the awesome temple-towers (in the form of terraced pyramids) of the ancient Babylonians and Assyrians, on top of which the gods were supposed to live.

**Nirvana**. Heaven for the Buddhists. It's more a state of mind than a place: the experience of becoming enlightened -- enjoying a blissful peace free of passions and suffering. The ego has melted away, and the soul joins with, communes with, the highest, ultimate reality -- the reality known to God. At this towering height of awareness, reincarnation isn't needed anymore.

**Nisroc**. Hell's top dietician, according to occult folklore of the Middle Ages. His culinary specialty: He likes to add the fruit of Eden's forbidden Tree of Immortality to his hellish dishes. (Before he fell and took up kitchen work, Nisroc had stood guard over the Tree.)

**Og**. See Nephilim.

**Padre Pio**.  As a young Roman Catholic priest, the famous Padre Pio went into ecstasies in which he allegedly conversed out loud with Jesus, Mary, his guardian angel, and St. Francis, often in a light banter, while others took notes on what was said, according to Fr. Allesio Parente in the book *Send Me Your Guardian Angel*.

The Italian priest also was known for his suggestion that people needing spiritual help or prayer send him their guardian angels -- if they could not come in person.  These angel missions are said to have brought satisfying results to the petitioners.  An associate of Padre Pio reported that the priest complained one morning that a steady succession of arriving guardian angels with different requests the night before had kept him awake all night.

One man who felt unable to resist peer pressure to join a robbery reportedly sent his guardian angel to the padre and then "by coincidence," a police car appeared in the area, foiling the robbery scheme.

However, during the course of the padre's ministry, the angel traffic was actually two-way: Padre Pio reportedly sent his own guardian angel (whom he described as petite) out on errands to help others, if only to give them a feeling of comfort.

In 1918, Pio received the *stigmata* -- an appearance of bleeding wounds on the body like those of Christ's on the cross.

Pio's guardian angel was supposedly an "angel of all trades," who translated foreign letters for him, repeatedly woke up his oversleeping companion Parente by knocking at his door -- and even once allegedly chauffeured a man, Piergiogio Biavatti (a friend of Parente's), for three hours in a car while Biavatti was sleeping at the wheel, Parente asserted.

Padre Pio's fame spread widely, and around the time of mass, the priest had to be careful lest worshipers with scissors cut his habit to pieces in a quest for relics. When the popular padre died in 1968, almost 100,000 people attended his funeral.

**Pahaliah**. An angel whom kabbalists invoked to turn unbelievers into Christians.

**Penemue**. In the ancient *Ethiopic Book of Enoch*, Penemue is the fallen angel who taught humankind the forbidden knowledge of writing. Noah, who describes this breach of the cosmic rules, says ruefully that Penemue "instructed mankind in writing with ink and paper, and thereby many sinned from eternity to eternity and until this day." Did the seafaring patriarch foresee yellow journalism and poison pen biographers?

**Pen-Ming**. This is a guardian spirit assigned to a newly ordained master in the major Chinese religion of Taoism. The pen-ming's job is to be a go-between for the master, delivering his prayers and his documents to the rulers of the universe, according to Peter Lamborn Wilson in his book *Angels*.

An angel stirs the water of the healing Pool of
Bethesda, mentioned in the Gospel of John.

**Pestilence Angel**. In the Bible's Book of 1 Chronicles, this is an unnamed sword-wielding angel sent by God to punish King David for conducting a census to find out how many people lived in Israel -- perhaps considered by the Lord to be unnecessary bureaucratic snooping. According to the legend, a displeased God gave David a chance to choose his "medicine" -- three years of famine for Israel, three months of military defeats or three days of killing disease. David declined to make a clear choice. Then, the punishment started -- an epidemic. The Lord sent an angel of pestilence who immediately killed 70,000 Israelites. Next, the angel turned its attention to Jerusalem. But, luckily, God changed his mind at the last minute, just as the angel was drawing his terrible sword, hovering in mid-air, ready to infect the population of the Holy City.

**Phanuel**. See Throne Angels.

**Philangeli** (Friends of Angels). A Catholic prayer organization founded in England in 1950 in honor of the angels. Today, it has members worldwide.

**Physical Intervention**. Sometimes angelic intervention is far more than the subtle "still, small voice within" or even a startling telepathic voice. Intervention can be as dramatic as a shove, a yank, a supporting hand when we falter, or even the lifting of a vehicle from one dangerous place to be set down at another, safe location -- according to those who have experienced this common phenomenon.

Typical is Eileen E. Freeman's story in her book *Touched by Angels*: In 1970, as a college student, Freeman was about to climb the steps leading to an apartment building where she was to meet a friend. "Suddenly, I felt a strong hand on my left shoulder that effectively brought me to a dead stop." Looking but seeing no one around, Freeman tried again to advance up the steps. But this time, the invisible hand not only stopped her but nearly pulled her backwards, and a voice said to her: "It would not be wise for you to go in there just now."

So, Freeman decided to wait a few more minutes by visiting a church across the street for a private devotion and a chance to think about the startling thing that had just happened. From the sanctuary, she heard approaching sirens. When she looked outside, she saw four police and emergency vehicles and police officers, with guns drawn, racing inside. She learned later from her friend that a drug dealer had stabbed to death a woman in an elevator inside the apartment building.

"If my angel hadn't warned me, I might have been the one who was killed," Freeman wrote.

Equally dramatic is the account of Cheri Leslie of Fourth Dimension Bookstore in Venice, Calif., a story appearing in Terry Lynn Taylor's *Answers From the Angels*: As a young woman, according to Leslie, her marriage was in tatters, her life chaotic, and she found herself in deep depression. "Late one night, feeling alone and desperate, I contemplated suicide," she wrote. "With a kitchen knife before me, I laid my head on the table and collapsed in tears, crying to God for help. There was an immediate presence that enveloped me, lifting me from my chair.

Holding and supporting my body, this presence led me to the drawer to put the knife away and then up the stairs to bed."

**Poetry about Angels**. One of literature's most famous poems concerning angels is the Italian Dante Alighieri's *Divine Comedy*, an imaginary tale of his journey through hell, purgatory and finally heaven, written in the 1300s. (See Dante) Another is *Paradise Lost*, the greatest adventure poem in the English language -- a 12-volume epic about the War in Heaven between good and bad angels at the dawn of time, Satan's revenge against God by tempting and corrupting Adam and Eve, and humankind's salvation later on. (See Milton, John). A sampling of other angel poetry:

■ The romantic 19th poet Lord Byron: "The angels all were singing out of tune/ And hoarse from having little else to do/ Excepting to wind up the sun and moon/ Or curb a runaway young star or two."

■ The abolitionist author of *Uncle Tom's Cabin*, Harriet Beecher Stowe: "Sweet Souls around us watch us still/ Press nearer to our side/ Into our thoughts, into our prayers/ With gentle helpings glide."

■ In Leigh Hunt's famous poem about Abou Ben Adhem, the hero "awoke one night from a deep dream of peace" to discover a recording angel by his bedside, scribbling in a golden book to make a report on Abou to God. When the angel asked if Abou had any suggestions, Abou thought a moment, then said: "Write me as one who loves his fellow man." The angel returned the next night to show that Abou's name was now at the top of God's honor roll.

■ Recluse Victorian poetess Emily Dickinson: "We trust, in plumed procession/ For such the angels go/ Rank after rank, with even feet/ And uniforms of snow."

■ The Romantic poet William Wordsworth: "What know we of the Blest above/ But that they sing, and that they love?")

**Polls and Angels**. Polling consistently shows that persons who have angelic encounters or extraordinary visions are by no means a lunatic fringe. On the contrary, they represent a substantial minority within the larger population.

In the early 1980s, Dutch surgeon Hans Moolenburgh randomly surveyed 400 of his patients, asking each if he or she had ever seen an angel. At least eight percent said yes, and Moolenburgh's results got major news coverage in Holland. One woman told how an invisible force lifted her bicycle and moved it through the air to keep a German panzer from crushing her during the Nazi blitzkrieg of 1940.

Moolenburgh's percentage is not at all unusual. For example, a 1990 Gallup poll had 13 percent of respondents saying that they had had an encounter with an angel, a devil, or some other kind of supernatural experience. In the same poll, half of the American population, and three quarters of teens expressed belief that angels exist.

In 1987, the Rev. Ben Johnson, a Lutheran minister with a Harvard doctorate, surveyed 14 Roman Catholic and Protestant congregations in St. Cloud, Minn. In the 2,000 responses collected in that city of 45,000, 30 percent reported having had an extraordinary experience, ranging from hearing heavenly voices and seeing religious visions to experiencing visitations and prophetic dreams. Johnson commented: "Two centuries after the intellectual world has said that this kind of thing does not happen, they show up among almost a third of the population in a conservative Midwestern city."

On another front, pollsters estimate that eight to nine million Americans have had a mystical near-death experience of one type or another.

Some of the most striking otherworldly surveying has been done by the famous Roman Catholic priest, sociologist and novelist, Fr. Andrew Greeley. As early as 1973, Fr. Greeley conducted a scientific poll for the National Opinion Research Center (NORC) at the University of Chicago, in which a representative sampling of 1,467 Americans was asked this question: "Have you ever felt that you were in touch with someone who died?" No less than 27 per cent said yes. And even more sobering, the percentage shot up from 27 to 51 among widows and widowers, who reported contact with dead spouses.

Later, a mid-1980s poll by NORC showed even higher numbers. In that survey, four out of 10 Americans said they had been in contact with someone dead, while 67 percent of widows and widowers said they had experienced contact with dead spouses. In the same poll, 31 percent said they had been clairvoyant at some point. Writing in *American Health* magazine, Fr. Greeley concluded: "What was paranormal is now normal."

**Population of Angels**. Whatever their numbers, angels have generally been believed by philosophers to outnumber mortals about like the Sioux nation outnumbered Custer's Seventh Cavalry. After all, the more perfect the creatures, the more of them, many churchmen have believed. Some people, though, have wanted an exact halo count: Jewish mystics in the Middle Ages turned words into numbers and back again to come up the precise figure of 301,655,722, roughly the population of the former Soviet Union. But the English playwright of the 1600s, Thomas Heywood, warned that zealots counting angels down to the last pair of sandals would just "grow from ignorance to error."

**Postage Stamp Angels**. A natural starting point for collectors of angels on stamps has been Vatican City, the tiny, independent "postage stamp" state of 108.7 acres in the heart of the city of Rome (a country about the size of a city park). Ruled by the pope, this state has its own flag, coinage, and stamps, and for years, the airmail stamps all had angels on them.

Writing in the November-December 1992 *Angel-Watch* newsletter, editor Eileen Freeman, herself a collector of angel stamps, notes that thousands of postage stamps from around the world feature angels, some with interesting stories behind them, including one airmail stamp showing angels carrying a house through the air. That stamp, Freeman says, refers to a medieval Catholic legend that Jesus became upset that the house his mother had lived in at Nazareth had fallen into the hands of Moslems.

So Jesus instructed angels to fly the house to Christian Italy, to a spot called Loretto, which became a mecca, if you will, for pilgrims.

In 1990, angel stamps went political, becoming a weapon in a power struggle in Eastern Europe. That year, according to *Catholic Twin Circle*, the small Baltic Sea state of Lithuania, struggling to assert its independence from the then-Soviet Union, issued its first independent postage stamps since it was conquered by Stalin in 1940 -- five- and 10-kopek stamps showing an angel holding a lamp against a backdrop of a map of Lithuania. But it wasn't until Communism collapsed in the Soviet Union in 1991 that Lithuania really broke free of Kremlin control. Incidentally, the patron of stamp collectors and postal services is none other than the great messenger archangel Gabriel.

**Powers**. The sixth-highest of the nine orders of angels in the Roman Catholic Church's traditional belief. They help keep the laws of the universe working so that, for example, the force holding an electron spinning around an atomic nucleus is just right. Change that force slightly, let atoms fly apart, and physical life would be impossible in the new, totally different universe. (See Pseudo-Dionysius)

**Princes**. The seventh of nine orders of angels in the Roman Catholic Church's traditional belief system. Princes stand guard over nations and leaders like the pope. They govern the rise and fall of nations. They protect good spirits from attack by jealous evil spirits. (See Pseudo-Dionysius)

**Pseudo-Dionysius**. About 500 years after Christ, a mysterious Middle Eastern writer calling himself Dionysius examined the Bible's scattered mentionings of angel names -- from the cherubim angels with flaming swords at the Garden of Eden to the six-winged seraph angel that pressed a burning coal to the lips of the prophet Isaiah. From these isolated stories, he somewhat arbitrarily cooked up a heavenly hierarchy of nine angel classes: from guardian angels, the lowest order, to burning seraphs, the highest. Unfortunately, this Middle Eastern writer signed his works *Dionysius*. And ancient Christians jumped to the conclusion that Dionysius was a famous early Christian by the same name -- a Greek judge mentioned in the Bible's Book of Acts. As a result, the mystery writer's theory of angel organization was very widely accepted in the Middle Ages -- until scholars finally proved his manuscripts were written centuries after the real Dionysius lived. For this reason, scholars today call our mystery writer by the quaint names of *Pseudo-Dionysius* or *False-Dionysius*. Nevertheless, Dionysius' hierarchy is still the most popular theory of angel organization in Christendom, although it faces a truckload of competing systems.

**Purgatory**. In the Middle Ages, Catholic Christians began to believe that a place of suffering called Purgatory exists -- a kind of spiritual "half-way house" for purging moderately sinful Christians of their iniquity in the afterlife, in preparation for their admission to heaven. Today, Catholics offer prayers which are believed to be helpful to the souls who are in

Purgatory. Protestant doctrine rejects Purgatory, but Orthodox Christians in the eastern churches believe that this realm exists.

**Putti**. The little winged youngster cherubs often seen hovering around in works of religious art. In the popular mind, cherubs have gone from being thought of 3,000 years ago as monstrous winged lions with human heads guarding ancient buildings to being drawn today as chubby winged babes on Christmas cards tooting silver trumpets. Quite an evolution!

**Quodlibets**. Subtle mind games in which angel scholars of the Middle Ages logically debated the very fine points of angels. The most famous quodlibet is: "How many angels can dance on the point of a needle?" Answer: All the angels in God's universe can. This is because angels, some philosophers argue, have no matter or mass and therefore take up no space. Another brain teaser was: "If ghostly angels take on physical bodies when they appear on earth to mortals (like a job applicant donning a suit for an interview) -- what happens to the 'body' when the angel goes back to heaven."

**Quotations About Angels**. Many of the most popular quotations concerning angels come, naturally, from the Bible:
■ "Remember to welcome strangers in your homes. There were some who did that and welcomed angels without knowing it. (Hebrews 13:2)
■ "God will put his angels in charge of you to protect you wherever you go." (Psalm 91:11)

■ "See that you don't despise any of these little ones. Their angels in heaven, I tell you, are always in the presence of my Father in heaven." (Jesus, quoted in Matthew 18:10)

Often-cited or interesting secular quotations include:

■ "Angels can fly because they take themselves lightly." The popular turn-of-the-century writer Gilbert Chesterton.

■ "Is man an ape or an angel? I, my lord, I am on the side of the angels. I repudiate with indignation and abhorrence those newfangled theories (of evolution)." The Victorian British Prime Minister Benjamin Disraeli.

■ "It is not because angels are holier than men or devils that makes them angels, but because they do not expect holiness from one another, but from God alone." William Blake, the visionary poet-artist of the late 1700s and early 1800s who said he saw angels in trees as a child.

■ "Goodnight, sweet prince, and flights of angels sing thee to thy rest." Horatio's farewell to his dead friend Hamlet in the Shakespeare play *Hamlet*.

■ "...we create what we believe. Indeed, I am prepared to say that if enough of us believe in angels, then angels exist," Gustav Davidson in the introduction to his *Dictionary of Angels*.

■ "To equip a dull, respectable person with wings would be a parody of an angel." The famous Victorian novelist, essayist and poet Robert Louis Stevenson.

■ "Angels keep their ancient places; Turn but a stone and start a wing!" Turn-of-the-century English poet Francis Thompson.

■ "That's all an angel is -- an idea of God." The medieval German mystic Johannes (Meister) Eckhart.

■ "Angels and ministers of grace defend us!" Hamlet's exclamation on seeing the ghost of his father in the Shakespeare play *Hamlet*.

■ "Our acts our angels are, or good or ill, our fatal shadows that walk by us still." The English playwright John Fletcher in *The Honest Man's Fortune* (1613).

■ "Angels aren't perfectionists... As G.K. Chesterton said: 'Angels can fly because they take themselves lightly.' In contrast, the devil -- aspiring to perfection -- fell on account of his gravity."
*F. Forrester Church*, pastor of All Souls Church in Manhattan.

**Raguel**. (Friend of God). As heaven's class monitor, Raguel keeps watch over the behavior of his fellow angels. This tough job no doubt called for long hours, considering how often angels have turned out to be easy marks for corrupting temptation. By some accounts, it was also Raguel who carried Enoch to heaven.

**Rahab**. (The Violent Angel) During Creation, God was separating the waters of the cosmos to make a dry spot for the earth to be placed in. God ordered the angel Rahab, as Prince of the Sea, to swallow all of the world's water. Rahab unwisely told God to leave him alone, and God kicked him to death. Rahab's carcass stank so horribly that nothing on earth could stand the stench, so God submerged the corpse below the ocean.

(Ancient Jews thought that the sky was a solid dome, and the nighttime stars were like little peepholes into the bright heaven behind the dark dome. Above the dome was water, and sometimes, the angels allowed these upper waters to sprinkle down through the peepholes to earth as rain. Under the flat earth were the lower waters.)

Despite his horrible death, Rahab shows up alive and kicking in a later legend -- but having, understandably, changed jobs. This time, Rahab is busy trying to stop Moses and his Hebrew slaves from escaping Egypt's Pharaoh by moving across the Red Sea during the Exodus. For this second no-no, Rahab was again destroyed.

**Raphael**. (God Heals). Tradition says that friendly Raphael specializes in healing, nurturing creativity, and guarding young people. He also supervises the guardian angels. (He is credited by some with healing Abraham of the pain of circumscion which the patriarch submitted to in his old age).

Raphael is believed to pay special attention to those who are trying to grow spiritually or make religious pilgrimages. So artists often show Raphael as a traveler, carrying a walking stick and a water gourd. Indeed, Raphael helped the traveling Tobias ward off the demon Asmodeus, according to Bible legend (See Asmodeus). Raphael is also known for his sense of humor.

Acting in his role as the guardian angel of the human race, particularly watchful over the young and innocent, it was Raphael who warned Adam (in vain) about the danger of sin, according to Christian folklore. In Puritan poet John Milton's famous *Paradise Lost*, this angel friend of humanity even took the time to eat supper with Adam and Eve in the Garden of Eden.

During the meal, Raphael turned red with embarrassment because he had to explain how the angels make love, even though they all have the appearance of males. Raphael explains to Adam that, actually, the angel body of finer matter can take on the identity of either gender, or even both. Sex is a matter of merging their spirit bodies. However, this "angel sex," some commentators suggest, is not an erotic coupling, but rather a spiritual union -- an agape bonding.

Meanwhile, folklore even has Raphael helping with construction. In the mythical Jewish *Testament of Solomon*, the archangel gives King Solomon a magic ring which the sage monarch uses to force a slave army of demons to finish building the Temple in Jerusalem.

**Rashnu**. (Righteousness) The stern but upright angel who judges the newly dead souls in the ancient Persian religion of Zoroastrianism.

After a person's death, his soul has to cross the Cinvat Bridge to get from this world to heaven, but there stands Rashnu, the bridge's guardian, blocking the way. For three days, the soul waits beside its corpse while Rashnu ponders his verdict on how the person has spent his life on earth. Rashnu weighs the worthiness of the soul in golden scales so sensitive and accurate that they do not deviate by a hair's breadth. A good person, passing muster, is helped by a comely maiden in the difficult crossing over this transitional bridge. But the wicked person finds that the already challenging bridge becomes far worse, as narrow as a razor's edge. Getting no help, he falls off and plummets downward to devils waiting below to torture him.

(Zoroastrianism's ideas of heaven and hell and a Last Judgment were borrowed by Judaism, which in turn passed this thinking on to Christianity. For the original Jewish idea of the afterlife, see Sheol.)

**Raziel**. (God Is My Pleasure) According to Jewish rabbi folklore, the wise angel Raziel took pity on Adam and Eve after they were driven out of the Garden of Eden. Standing behind the curtains that are drawn around the Throne of God, Raziel sees and hears everything. Therefore, savvy Raziel gave poor Adam *The Book of the Angel Raziel*, which contained all the knowledge of the universe. This formidable tome allowed Adam to look into the "mirror of existence" and see both God and himself in God's image. After being thrown into the sea by jealous angels and retrieved by the angel Rahab under God's order, the book eventually fell into the possession of the righteous Old Testament character Enoch, who fathered the world's oldest man, Methuselah. Enoch memorized the book, became one of the world's wisest men, and finally was swept up to heaven by God without having to die. Later, Noah got the book and used it as a guide for building his ark. Centuries after that, the Hebrew King Solomon used it to make powerful magic. After that, alas, the invaluable tome dropped out of sight.

**Remiel**. (God's Mercy) In Jewish folklore, Remiel seems to be confused about his loyalties, or is perhaps a double agent. In the *Book of Enoch*, Remiel is listed as one of the seven holy archangels who have the privilege of standing in God's immediate presence. And yet the same book elsewhere states that Remiel is one of the fallen angels!

**Resurgence of Angel Interest**. In the Middle Ages, angels were all the rage. Carved angels crowded churches' ornamentation. Believers kept diaries, called *fiorettis*, of times in their lives when angels intervened. Giants of literature stimulated medieval and early modern readers with tales of angel derring-do. The major English poet John Milton penned a 12-volume epic about angels fighting in heaven and the subsequent Fall of Man. Italy's foremost poet Dante wrote about a journey through hell, Purgatory and heaven. Philosophers spent long hours arguing about or analyzing angels' finer points: These subtle mind games of logic were called *quodlibets*, the most famous being, "How many angels can stand on the head of a pin?"

Then, something terrible happened to the angels. The intellectual leadership of the West started to believe that the physical is all there is -- and the universe nothing but a big, dead, purposeless random machine without any hidden spiritual world behind it (i.e., the philosophy of *scientific materialism*). In this climate of skepticism, interest in angels nosedived. Angels were now fit only to decorate Christmas card covers, and the very subject prompted not fascination, but an indulgent smile. As recently as the early 1980s, author Hans Moolenburgh wrote: "Angels are not found anymore, and that is a great pity... We have become just like people who have lost their shadow."

But even as Moolenburgh was writing -- happily, the seeds of changed thinking were already germinating. Scientific materialism was under heavy attack on fronts ranging from spreading Eastern mysticism to the bizarre picture of reality emerging from subatomic physics, and by the 1990s, the angels were once again ascending. In the bookstores, angel books underwent a population explosion as publishers reacted to a sudden, strong demand for them by readers. Hollywood stopped laughing at angels. Less visible was the cartoon-like image of the bumbling angel (such as Clarence Oddbody of the 1940s film classic *It's a Wonderful Life*). More serious and credible angels appeared onscreen -- like Jonathan Smith of the long-running prime-time TV series *Highway to Heaven*. And consider the film *Ghost*, about a murdered man who lingered on earth in spirit form to guard his wife against his attacker. *Ghost* was the number one grossing film in 1990.

By 1992, the escalating interest in angels was being trumpeted in the national media: in a front page story in The Wall Street Journal; a series of national wire stories by The Associated Press; a major story in USA Today. Angel authors were showing up on national talk shows. But why all this? How did angels resurrect themselves from the cultural grave? The most common explanation being offered was that the idea of angels is a comfort to people in the turbulent times of the late 20th Century. A less common, but intriguing, explanation put forward was that the West was changing its mind again about the basic nature of reality. Because of accumulating evidence, coming out of science itself, the philosophy of *scientific materialism* -- the idea that the physical is all there is -- was being abandoned in favor of a return to the idea that a spiritual world exists, undergirding the world of matter. In this new climate, angels could become not only plausible but exciting.

An angel shows John of Patmos the New Jerusalem coming down from heaven. (Gustave Dore illustration for the Book of Revelation)

**Ridwan**. The Moslem angel guarding the entrance of the terrestrial Paradise.

**Saints and Angels**. Bios of saints (*hagiographies*) abound with angelic encounters. A saint's spiritual purity, life of contemplation, and/or asceticism may make contact with higher realms more likely. Nevertheless, what actually happened in history has often been lost beneath a thick growth of legend or mythology. Here are a variety of angel-saint encounters:

■ St. Frances of Rome (1384-1440) allegedly received a "light blow heard by all" from her guardian angel when he was displeased with her.

■ St. Francisca, who lived in the 1400s, had a guardian angel whose face was so brilliantly white, she could read her midnight prayers by its glow.

■ During the 1500s, St. Teresa of Avila would occasionally see a vision of a short, beautiful angel with a flaming face and body, carrying a long, golden spear. During the vision, the angel would pierce St. Teresa's heart repeatedly with the spear, causing her to burn with a great love for God.

**Samael**. ("Poison") Samael is often synonymous with Satan, but sometimes he is a different personality -- an angel of death who brought mortality into the world. As an Angel of Death, Samael played a key role in the very tough time God had getting Moses to die, according to one tale recounted in Ginzberg's *Legends of the Jews* (Volume III). Moses was 120 years old and had led his people for 40 years through the Sinai wilderness to the brink of the Promised Land of Palestine. Now, it was time for him to die, and God looked around for a special angel to bring the soul of this spiritual giant to heaven.

The angels Gabriel, Michael and Zagzagel (Moses' teacher) all begged off the task. They didn't want the Lawgiver, who had been so righteous, to have to taste death at their hands. God, however, noted that he had forced other righteous patriarchs like Noah and Abraham to die. So finally, God turned to the specialist, Samael, Angel of Death. Unlike the others, Samael was delighted, grabbed his sword, got himself into a cruel frame of mind, and whisked himself off toward Moses.

But Moses' blindingly radiant face frightened Samael, and he fled back to God empty-handed, angering the Creator. God ordered Samael back to Moses, and the Lawgiver promptly beat Samael with his fabled staff (the one that had turned into a snake in front of pharaoh), and the angel was blinded. God himself next intervened, ordering Michael, Gabriel and Zagzagel to carry Moses' soul to the highest heaven on a couch. Moses at last obeyed God, but then his soul objected. Finally, God kissed Moses, and the enraptured soul leaped joyfully out of the body.

In another legend, Samael and other tempting angels disguised themselves as men and women and shamelessly put on a sex education display in front of Adam and Eve. The primal pair had just been ejected from the Garden of Eden and had no idea how to keep the human race going -- now that they had lost their immortality by eating the forbidden fruit. Fortunately, Adam told God what was happening, and God thwarted Samael by marrying Adam and Eve, according to the apocryphal *Book of Adam*.

**An angel drives Adam and Eve out of the Garden of Eden. (Gustave Dore illustration for the Book of Genesis)**

**Sandalphon**. ("Synadelphos?" = Colleague of Metatron) One legend says the heavenly secretary Metatron carries prayers up through 900 heavens to God. If the prayer is in Hebrew, says a different legend, the same Metatron teams up with twin brother Sandalphon to weave a garland out of it for God to wear on his head. Sandalphon is so tall, it would take 500 years to get from his feet to his scalp. In some folklore, it was believed that Israel's most popular prophet, Elijah, was turned into the angel Sandalphon after the Hebrew prophet was lifted up to heaven in a fiery chariot amid a whirlwind -- without having to die (2 Kings 2:11). In addition to other duties, Sandalphon, by some accounts, is in charge of birds.

**Satan**. (The Enemy) Once the greatest of the highest angels, the seraphim -- Satan served as God's viceroy, according to Christian folklore. He was the smartest and most glorious of the host. But he grew jealous and rebelled against his Maker when God created humanity and decided to unite with humankind in the person of Jesus Christ. Others say it was not envy, but arrogance that was the first sin. Interestingly, the early leaders of the Christian Church argued with themselves over whether Satan would find salvation in the end and return to God.

Medievals imagined the Father of Lies to have horns, a face behind him, cloven feet, and a stinking, hairy body, the theologian Geddes MacGregor has noted in his book *Angels: Ministers of Grace*. Yet the devil frequently disguised himself as a beautiful heavenly angel, or he might take on the form of an attractive maiden or youth to seduce someone. If it worked, he would become again his loathsome self and drag away the terrified victim to hell. In fact, medievals blamed virtually every mortal problem on Satan, even monastery choirs singing off key.

In Christian art, Satan had regular angel wings until around the 1100s, MacGregor reports. Then, more and more, he is shown with bat-like wings. Also, over the centuries, his originally depicted black skin came to be shown by artists as hellfire red. Christians consider Satan's foremost job to be tempting, and his foremost tools for temptation are money, power and sexual lust.

In Dante's *Divine Comedy*, Dante visits the bottom of hell, the lowest point in the universe, and sees a gigantic Satan, partly buried in a lake of ice, flapping bat-like wings and chewing on the world's three greatest sinners, Brutus and Cassius (the assassins of Julius Caesar), and Judas Iscariot. The ice symbolized Satan's monstrously frigid, unloving soul. In John Milton's *Paradise Lost*, Satan decides to corrupt Adam and Eve as a way of getting back at God for kicking him and the bad angels of out of heaven. Worst of all, to the jealous Satan, God was planning to repopulate the vacancies in heaven (caused by the loss of the bad angels) with human beings, after humans had had some time to become more moral and spiritual.

Some believe that Satan doesn't exist as an actual being, fighting God. Rather, in this theory, Lucifer is a symbol for evil, which exists like a cold shadow that contrasts with the warm light of spiritual love and understanding. Evil, then, would be the *absence* of God and His Goodness, rather than a thing or being in itself. In ancient Judaism, Satan (*ha-satan*), was not thought to be a rebel angel fighting God. In the Book of Job, for example, Satan acts as heaven's official tempter, a kind of harsh prosecutor who wants to make sure that believers are true to God by testing and tempting them. But this official tempter was always acting under God's authority and command, even if he was a "spy, stoolpigeon, agent provocateur, prosecutor, hangman," as the scholar Bernard Bamberger put it. Later, by the time of the New Testament era, thinking about Satan had changed. By that period of history, Christians were seeing him as an evil rebel angel fighting and disobeying God. Many scholars think that this change of mind began when the Jews came into contact with the Zoroastrian religion during their captivity in Babylon. Zoroastrianism was teaching that a good god and a devil were in a cosmic war with each other.

**Sariel**. (The Command of God) According to the *Book of Enoch* Sariel is one of the seven premier archangels. His job is to take responsibility for the destiny of those angels who have flouted God's Laws.

**Scriptural Angels**. The Bible names only three angels, Michael, Gabriel and Raphael. In the Old Testament Apocrypha (Old Testament Books mostly accepted by Catholics as fully scriptural but rejected by Protestants and Jews), Uriel and Jeremiel are named. The Koran names seven angels, Mikel (Michael); Djibril (Gabriel); Malik, the righteous but awful angel overseeing hell; Iblis, the Islamic devil; Harut and Marut, two angels who came to earth and were corrupted by its temptations; and the Angel of Death (Azrael).

**Sefiroth**. At the dawn of time, when God created the universe, he first radiated from himself 10 basic intelligences, according to certain Jewish mystics. Each of these intelligences represented a trait or characteristic of God. And together, these 10 creative powers control the universe, according to the mystical Jewish philosophy called Kabbalah, which peaked in popularity during the Middle Ages. God Himself is an infinite being who is so far above humans and his lower Creation that he is unknowable to us, even inconceivable, according to the Spanish kabbalistic book *Zohar* ("Brightness"). Since God is so "high up," so to speak, he uses the 10 *sefiroth* as intermediaries in dealing with and controlling his lower Creation. Most authorities identify the sefiroth as *Kether*, God's Will and his Thought; *Hokhmah*, God's plan for the universe; *Binah*, God's Intelligence; *Hesed*, Divine Love; *Gevurah*, Divine Judgment (God's unswerving justice); *Rahamin*, Divine Compassion (or *Tiphereth*, Beauty, in some systems); *Netsah*, Lasting Endurance or Eternity; *Hod*, Divine Majesty; *Yesod*, the Base of every activity in God; *Shekhinah*, the Presence of God. Kabbalists personified these Divine Traits as various archangels, including Metatron, Michael and Raphael.

**Semjaza**. According to the ancient *Book of Enoch*, Semjaza led 200 comrades from heaven to earth without God's permission to mate with beautiful mortal women. Apparently, they were driven to that by what the writer of *Enoch* calls their "privy members... like those of horses." Worse than the illicit sex, Semjaza's angels taught humans all kinds of forbidden and harmful knowledge.

Azazel, for example, taught men how to make weapons to wage war, and he taught women the vanity of cosmetics. Soon, the women gave birth to a race of gigantic hungry jacks -- some of them more than two miles tall. These chowdowns swallowed all the world's food, snacked on ordinary humans, and finally started cannibalizing each other.

When the earth was plunged into fornication and total anarchy, God sent down his powerful warrior angel Michael, and the lustful angels were imprisoned until doomsday in earth's valleys. The giants were killed, but evil spirits from their souls continued to torment the earth. God wiped out the giants by sending the Flood, but He first sent Uriel to warn Noah that it was coming.

**Seraphim**. The highest of the nine orders of angels in the Catholic Church's traditional belief. The seraphs are called the "burning ones" because they are closest to God, have the most perfect understanding of Him of all creatures, and therefore, they are aflame with love for Him. Pie-Raymond Regamy compares them to "moths madly beating with their wings against the glass of the lamp (the divine light of God) at which they would (gladly) burn themselves." Theologian Geddes MacGregor quotes the medieval mystic Jan van Ruysbroeck as saying that the very highest angels -- the seraphim, cherubim and thrones -- do not take part "in our struggle against our vices, but dwell with us only when, above all conflict, we are with God in peace, in contemplation, and in perennial love." (See Pseudo-Dionysius)

**Seven Archangels**. Heaven's elite. In the Bible's *Book of Revelation* and the *Book of Tobit*, these are the seven angels who are privileged to stand before the face of God, but they go unnamed. Usually, they are thought to be archangels. Most ancient writers thought that the angelic stars Gabriel, Michael, Raphael and Uriel made the team. Metatron, Raguel, Zadkiel and Raziel are among contenders to fill the berth's remaining three seats, with different sources favoring various angels.

**Seven Heavens**. In Hebrew myth, the seven heavens are vaulted above the earth, one on top of the other, like the skins of an onion -- except for the first and lowest heaven.

The first and lowest heaven is like a curtain drawn over the sky during the day, according to Ginzberg's *the Legends of the Jews* (Volume 1) and *Hebrew Myths* by Graves and Patai. This curtain heaven is rolled back at night to reveal the cosmos -- the higher heavens.

The planets are fastened to the second heaven. In the third heaven, mills are busy grinding out manna, the Biblical food of the wandering Jews escaping from slavery in Egypt and the food for the righteous in the hereafter. In the fourth heaven is the heavenly Jerusalem. Nightly angel choirs sing God's praises in the fifth heaven, but they quiet down at sunrise so God can hear Israel singing his praises during the day. The sixth heaven is stockpiled with woes to be inflicted on the earth, including lofts filled with noxious dew, storage bins holding storms, smoke-filled cellars, and so on.

In the seventh heaven is the Throne of God, the spirits of unborn generations, the souls of the righteous, and the dew that God will use to raise the dead on Resurrection Day.

According to the *Book of Enoch* mythology, during his tour of the seven heavens, the Old Testament patriarch Enoch saw storehouses of snow, ice, clouds and dew in the first heaven as well as 200 angels who rule the stars; in the second heaven, he saw sinners in chains as they await Judgment Day; in the third, Enoch saw the Garden of Eden with its Tree of Life and forbidden fruit, where God rests in the shade when he visits there; in the fourth, the sun and moon ride their chariots through the sky; in the fifth heaven, the doomed fallen angels were imprisoned. In the sixth, angels are studying astrology; and in the seventh is the Divine Throne.

The mystical Jewish book Zohar claims not seven heavens, but 390, along with 70,000 worlds.

**Seven Cardinal Sins and Their Respective Demons**. By some accounts, the pair-up is as follows: Arrogance - Lucifer; jealousy - Leviathan; laziness - Belphegor; lechery - Asmodeus; greed - Mammon; gluttony - Beelzebub; anger - Satan.

**Shaitans**. In the Moslem religion, angelic guards patrol the walls of heaven to prevent eavesdropping by such evil spirits as shaitans and djinn. One shaitan, however, a great-grandson of the Moslem devil Iblis, appeared one day before the prophet Mohammed. Mohammed taught this shaitan various chapters of the Koran, helping him begin to get right with God.

**Shamshiel**. In Hebrew myth, Shamshiel is the angel prince of the Garden of Eden. He once took Moses on a guided tour of the place, where the Lawgiver saw Abraham and other righteous persons sitting on 70 jeweled thrones.

**Shemhazai and Azazel**. (See Semyaza) Two angels who decided to brave the sinfulness of earth to show that they could remain uncontaminated in that tempting environment. It all started when a grieving God looked down at the evil and idolatrous last generation before the Flood, about to be destroyed by His hand. Shemhazai and Azazel came forward and reminded the Almighty that He had been warned by the angels about creating Man. God shot back that the angels would have done worse than man, had they had to live on the temptation-filled earth as humans had to, rather than in sinless heaven. Shemhazai and Azazel then bragged that they could do all right down there, and God told them to try. Alas, no sooner had the duo descended to earth than Shamhazai spotted a young virgin, Ishtar, and was filled with lust. "Grant my desire!" was his unambiguous opening line. Ishtar replied that that could be arranged, but only if Shamhazai first taught her how to pronounce the explicit name of God, allowing her to fly up to heaven. When she arrived in heaven, still sinless, having abandoned Shemhazai empty-handed, God rewarded her by placing her among the constellation of the seven stars called the Pleiades, to be remembered forever.

Meanwhile, Shemhazai and Azazel plunged into fornication with mortal women. Shemhazai begat the troublesome giants Hiva and Hiyya (the sorrowful Hebrew interjections: Woe! and Ah!).

For his part, Azazel set about teaching women how to use cosmetics to entice men to passion. Next, the angel Metatron, heaven's secretary, warned Shemhazai that God was about to flood the wicked earth and destroy both men and giants, sparing only the righteous Noah's family. Shemhazai was devastated by the news, constantly weeping over the coming doom of the earth and of his giant sons, whose appetite for food was cosmic. Heeva and Hiyya were also distressed, but God consoled them before their execution. The Lord told them that, after the Flood was over, their names, the sighing Hebrew exclamations Woe! and Ah!, would be uttered by the post-flood humans every time something wrong happened in the earth.

As for Shemhazai, he repented and hanged himself upside down between heaven and earth, where he remains, even today, still suspended as the constellation Orion. Azazel refused to be sorry about it all and is still around, trying to get women to use cosmetics and jewelry so men will be led astray. (The Jewish legend is presented by the scholar Leo Jung in his *Fallen Angels in Jewish, Christian and Mohammedan Literature*).

**Sheol**. (Hebrew: *Pit* or *Grave*) The ancient Hebrew hell, a vague shadowy land of the dead, similar to the netherworld Hades of the ancient Greeks. In this joyless realm (but not a place of punishment), dead mortals lose their individual identities and are merged together. Gradually, under the influence of the great ancient Persian religion Zoroastrianism, some Jews began to think that the individual soul lived on after death.

Also borrowed by the Jews was the Zoroastrian idea of a Final Judgment to separate good and bad souls for a blissful heaven or a tormenting, punishing hell. The new Jewish hell was called Gehenna. However, a bad soul's sentence to Gehenna was not life without parole, but a limited term, depending on how sinful the soul was. The Christian hell generally has been considered eternal, but there have been some important dissenters. For one, the great ancient Christian theologian Origen, probably the most able Biblical scholar of the ancient church, taught that even hell was a temporary place for purifying souls.

**Socrates' Daimon**. The ancient Greek philosopher Socrates claimed he had a personal guardian spirit, his "daimon," which warned him of trouble beforehand but never bossed him. On one occasion, this never-erring spirit cautioned Socrates against turning a particular corner. When his friends ignored the philosopher, they were suddenly shaken up and knocked down by a group of pigs.

**Sophia**. The angel whose foolishness was responsible for the creation of the physical world, a cosmic disaster which ended up leaving millions of human souls trapped on the physical plane and separated from a faraway God, too distant and too high up to help them. Here is how it happened, according to one version of the ancient religion of *gnosticism* reported by scholar G. Quispel: Sophia was the youngest of the *aeons* (gnostic angels) -- a rash youth who became arrogant and wanted to understand the unknowable vastness of God. As a result, she fell from heaven and found herself in a terrible emptiness, where no knowledge at all could be found. There, she was consumed with negative emotions -- passion, despair, fear, etc.

But she could still remember what the higher heavenly world was like. And as she recalled heaven, she brought forth Jesus into existence. Jesus asked the other aeons to rescue Sophia. The aeons then stripped her of all the negativity that tormented her. But the nasty "stuff" cleaned out of Sophia became the building blocks used to create the lower layers of the universe, including the physical world.

The negative physical world came under the control of the devil. Above the physical world, but still on a low level, was the psychic world, ruled by Yahweh, the ancient Hebrew god, who tended to be negative. Up farther, above the planets, were the happy, higher heavens of the universe, where Sophia and the good aeons lived close to the unknowable God.

**Spirit Guide**. A catchall term for an entity that watches over a person. Sometimes it may refer to an angel, or a departed mortal looking after loved ones, the higher self, or a being of another nature.

**Sraosha**. (To Hearken) An all-hearing Zoroastrian angel, who listened for complaints by earthly mortals of wrongdoing and mischief at the hands of evil-doers. Every night, when evil-doing tends to pick up momentum, Sraosha makes it his business to come down to earth in person in order to chase after Aesthma, the demon of violence and anger.

Because of his importance, Sraosha is allowed to stand in front of Ahura Mazda, the supreme spirit of goodness, in Ahura Mazda's heavenly court.

**Steiner, Rudolf**. (1861-1925) An Austrian philosopher and lecturer who developed detailed opinions about how the angel world operates. Around the turn of the century, Steiner attracted a following for these beliefs and for his metaphysical ideas in general. Steiner's system has nine ranks of creatures below the Trinity and above humankind: The seraphim (called "Spirits of Love"); the cherubim ("Spirits of the Harmonies"); the Thrones ("Spirits of Will"); Kyriotetes ("Spirits of Wisdom"); Dynamis ("Spirits of Movement"); Exusiai ("Spirits of Form"); Archai ("Spirits of Personality"); Archangels ("Fire-Spirits"); and Angels ("Sons of Life"). In 1913, Steiner founded the Anthroposophical Society as an organization for furthering his philosophy.

**Suffix Angels**. Angels existing in name only, just on paper. Imaginative ancient and medieval writers created thousands of these empty angels out of thin air (without any real traditions behind them) just by adding the two angel-making word endings "-el" and "-irion" to ordinary words in Hebrew (usually Hebrew nouns) -- and sometimes joining the suffix to foreign words.

One writer took the Hebrew word for hail, *Barad*, added -el, and created *Baradiel*, the fallen angel in the *Book of Enoch*, who presumably would preside over hailstones. Another bad habit contributing to the runaway angel birth rate was the practice of snatching gods from foreign religions and adding the ubiquitous

-*el* to make a new angel. In this way, the angel-like Greek god Hermes became the angel *Hermesiel*. So, too, the Babylonian god of death Nergal was kidnapped into Judaism to become Nasargiel, guiding Moses on a tour of the underworld in one tale. In those uncritical times, if a new angel just hung around long enough in the literature, it often had an excellent chance of being accepted. The upshot of these and other angel-making practices: Soon there was a winged creature governing well nigh everything under the sun -- a situation perhaps getting too close to polytheism for comfort. At any rate, Pope Zachary and a Church Council cracked down on this population explosion in 745 A.D. The council declared that no angels were to be called on for help except the three mentioned in the Bible by name, Michael, Gabriel and Raphael. Even some big name angels like Uriel, the angel of prophecy and interpretation, were denounced by the no-nonsense council as false. The most popular angel-making suffix, -el, means "God" in Hebrew.

**"Still, Small Voice."** That subtle, intuitive feeling or knowing that comes from within. We get the phrase from the Old Testament story in which the Hebrew prophet Elijah climbed the holy Mt. Sinai. Then, the Lord passed by Elijah and sent a furious wind, next an earthquake and finally a fire. But the Lord was not present in any of those thunderous events. However, in the ensuing calm, there came to Elijah "a still, small voice," the voice of God whispering to the prophet -- rather than thundering down to him from on high.

Where does that quiet voice, that subtle feeling, come from that whispers to us from within, advising us, warning us, giving us a superior insight, a wisdom that does not seem to come from ourselves? Some see in this inner intuition the subtle urging of an outside guardian angel. Others argue that the limited conscious mind is tapping its much greater subconscious depths. Whatever the source, it is often said that there is a "use it or lose it" principle at work here: The helpful voice of intuition strengthens if its beneficiary has the courage to heed the guidance he is given (after being sure the guidance was truly heavensent), but the guidance weakens if ignored.

"A sort of circulation of the blood is set up with heaven," writes Hans Moolenburgh in *A Handbook of Angels*. "You ask for guidance, then you get an answer. You carry out the suggestion, and you get further support when carrying out the task." But ignoring what you're told "blocks the channels," Moolenburgh adds.

**Summa Theologica**. Written in the 1200s by one of the Christian Church's greatest theologians, Thomas Aquinas, the so-called "Angelic Doctor," this massive tome gives a microscopically detailed description of the angel life as Aquinas believed it to be. (Many other theological subjects are also covered in other sections of the hefty book).

Using his logic and reasoning ability as glue, Aquinas cobbled together doctrines and speculations about the angel world that had gradually accumulated in the Christian Church for more than a millennium. Most of these opinions came from Augustine (the main authority in Aquinas' day for Western

**The Hebrew patriarch Abraham encounters three angels. (Gustave Dore illustration)**

theologians), Pope Gregory the Great (who popularized Augustine) and pseudo-Dionysius (creator of the most popular theory of angel organization in the Christian world). In his *Summa*, Aquinas expressed the opinion (not without dissenters) that angels are minds without bodies, purely intellectual beings. And he said that each individual angel is as different from another as one species of creature is from another.

**Superstitions About Angels**. The Irish say that a child smiling in its sleep is having a talk with angels. But to the Armenians, that snoozing cherubic smile actually comes from the fact the child's guardian angel is tickling him by cutting his fingernails. Meanwhile, the French originated the saying that a sudden lull in a conversation is caused by an angel passing through. In Latin America, it was an old custom, if someone died, to hang black curtains over all mirrors so that the Angel of Death would not see his reflection. Medievals believed they could chase away demons by ringing church bells.

**Swedenborg, Emanuel**. One of the world's top scientists of the 1700s, Swedenborg in his 50s began going into trances lasting for days at a time during which he claimed to be visiting the spirit world. He said that maturing human souls gradually become angels in the afterlife. But at first, after death, an ordinary soul lives in a semi-physical world. This world is, at least partly, a "state of mind."

Swedenborg asserted that newly dead souls go right on feeling and thinking and doing a moment after death just as they did a moment before death.

In fact, things are so similar that some newly dead souls are "told by the angels" that they have become spirits. What's more, everything the human soul did or thought while it was on earth is revealed "before the angels in a light as clear as day."

The newly dead souls eventually go to the "place" that best suits their way of thinking, high, middlebrow or low. Heaven and hell are created by the states of mind -- the attitudes -- of those who voluntary gravitate to each realm. And so, Swedenborg's hell is "hellish" because it is voluntarily populated by darker personalities who freely indulge the vices and evils they became accustomed to on earth.

Swedenborg's contemporaries considered him insane. But soon after Swedenborg died at 84 just before the American Revolution an ocean away, his followers in England founded a church based on his teachings. Its members number 100,000 worldwide today and have included Helen Keller.

Swedenborg's comeback to his detractors: "I am well aware that many will say that no one can possibly speak with spirits and angels as long as he lives in the body... But by all this I am not deterred, for I have seen, I have heard, I have felt."

**Thought-Forms**. Are guardian angels, at least a certain number of them, really "thought forms," as some suggest, rather than normal beings? There is a controversial theory in the psychic community that habitually nurtured thoughts can take on a life of their own and begin wielding influence on the person whose mind brought them into existence, and on others. They become entities of sorts living in the non-physical world for a time, according to this theory.

Novelists sometimes report that their characters often take on an uncanny life of their own, soon dictating to the author what they will do or say. Psychoanalyst Nandor Fodor, in his *Encyclopedia of Psychic Science*, quotes James T. Fields in a lecture Fields gave on *Fiction and its Eminent Authors*: "Dickens (the famous Victorian author of *A Christmas Carol, Oliver Twist*, and other works) was at one time so taken possession of by the characters of whom he was writing that they followed him everywhere and would never let him be alone for a moment."

Napoleon Hill, one of the greatest self-help authors of the 20th Century, noted that he once created in his imagination a group of imaginary counselors, whom he picked from among the great men of history, including Abraham Lincoln and Thomas Paine. Hill's original purpose was to concentrate on them and their biographies and gradually pick up some of the traits that had made them successful. But Hill reported that, after a time, these characters became extremely vivid in his imagination and began acting on their own. Hill began to worry that he would "lose sight of" the fact that they were merely a part of his imagination, and he dropped the practice of visualizing them for a time. Later, though, more confident, he returned to the practice and said that this council frequently gave him excellent advice.

**Throne Angels.** In the *Slavonic Book of Enoch*, the angels of the divine Throne are Michael, Gabriel, Uriel and Raphael, although in two other places in the same book, Phanuel subs for Uriel.

**Thrones**. The third-highest of the nine orders of angels in the Church's traditional belief. The job of the thrones is to consider the disposition of God's decisions. They are often pictured as fiery wheels. This is because the Old Testament prophet Ezekial saw them that way around 580 B.C., according to a Bible legend. Ezekial's vision began when he noticed a windstorm and thunderhead coming in from the north -- with the sky around it glowing. Within the storm were four human-like creatures, although each had four faces. They were also winged and had hooves. As the creatures darted around, lightning-quick, they were accompanied by four shining wheels, with rims that were "covered with eyes." Some commentators have speculated that what Ezekial saw was not angels, but UFOs. (See Pseudo-Dionysius)

**Traffic Angels**. Angels as traffic cops? The highways and byways seem to be particularly common arenas for heavenly beings to intervene, whether they be celestial angels or departed loved ones merely acting as "guardian angels." Some typical categories:

■ A voice warning the motorist to stop at an intersection despite a green light. A split-second later, another vehicle races out of a sidestreet and shoots illegally through the intersection.

■ "Road service" for a stranded motorist. Because of the unusualness of the helper, the driver is left convinced that the Good Samaritan was an angel in disguise (See Angels Disguised).

■ Accounts of vehicles being physically lifted up and moved out of harm's way.

- Vehicles avoiding head-on crashes when space to do so, it is realized afterward, simply was not available (for example, a narrow bridge).

Here are some illustrative stories:

- Around 1980, an elderly Florida widow was on the road when a large car hauling a boat suddenly darted into her path. She found herself paralyzed with fear as her car slid toward what looked to be a serious collision. At that point, she told me matter-of-factly, her late husband, dead for three months, materialized in her car.

"I was upset because I knew I was dying. I didn't see any way I could avoid a collision." Then, she said, her deceased husband just appeared in the car and steered the vehicle into a ditch, out of harm's way. All the time, the solid-looking apparition said nothing. Then, her husband vanished as mysteriously as he had appeared. "My mouth was gaping. I must have sat there for 20 minutes afterward, I was so shook up." She adds: "He's still my guardian angel."

- On a talk show where I once appeared in Birmingham, a caller phoned in to say he was traveling one day on a freeway in the Washington D.C. area when he heard a mental voice telling him to get out of his lane. When the voice spoke up a second time, he finally braked his car and began to leave the lane. At that point, he noticed a tractor-trailer topping a rise just in front of him, going the wrong way down the thoroughfare. The trucker braked his rig and a collision was narrowly avoided.

- In the summer 1989 issue of *Spiritual Frontiers*, William E. Clark recalled how, as a teen-ager in the 1930s he was driving some fellow football players home from a Friday afternoon game.

Clark's vehicle moved onto a single lane bridge. When Clark was about a third of the way across the bridge, a speeding pickup truck entered the bridge at the other end, and it seemed that a terrible head-on crash was unavoidable. "There was a blur of motion, and the truck was behind us continuing in the opposite direction." Yet Clark had felt nothing and heard no sound of impact. Clark's football coach and some other players following behind Clark in another vehicle (but stopping before entering the bridge) had witnessed the strange incident -- in broad daylight. Clark and the youth sitting beside him were mystified. On Sunday, that youth "came to my house to tell me that he and his father had driven to the bridge and measured its width; he said there was no possibility that two vehicles could meet and pass on that bridge."

**Tsadkiel**. Who passes out the standard-issue white robes and sandals in heaven? In kabbalistic (mystical Jewish) lore, Tsadkiel is heaven's quartermaster of clothing, issuing new outfits to the arriving souls. His overall job title is angel of justice, although Tsadkiel's duties are as varied as governing the planet Jupiter and, at one time, protecting Abraham, the father of the Jewish race.

**Uretil**. See Metatron.

**Uriel** (God's Light) The archangel Uriel is folklore's angel of prophecy and interpretation, an inspiration to writers and teachers. His symbols are a book and a scroll. Uriel's big name as an interpreter comes from his appearance in the apocryphal Old Testament Book 2 Esdras.

There, the Hebrew prophet Ezra has seven visions that are explained by Uriel to mean that a Jewish Messiah will come to crush evil. By some accounts, Uriel, wearing the hat of angel of prophecy, was the one who warned Noah that the Flood was coming. Meanwhile, Uriel also is in charge of natural phenomena, like earthquakes, thunderstorms and erupting volcanoes. In addition, legend has him as the ruler of the sun. Yet despite the blinding light of Old Sol, he is supposed to be the most eagle-eyed of the angels.

In the *Apocalypse of St. Peter*, Uriel mercilessly deals with blasphemers, who are strung up by their tongues over an unquenchable fire. In John Milton's *Paradise Lost*, Uriel is the governor of the sun and plays a key role in the tragic chain of events leading to the Fall of Man. In Milton's 12-volume tale, Satan vows revenge after he and his bad angels are kicked out of the sky, losing the War in Heaven. The best way to get back, he decides, is to corrupt God's newest creation, Adam and Eve -- but he lacks directions to their home, the Garden of Eden on earth. So Satan disguises himself as a young cherub, flies to the sun, tricks Uriel into giving him directions and then heads for earth. Uriel later figures out he was tricked and slides down on a ray of sunlight to the gate of Paradise, to tip off Gabriel and his angelic guard posted at Eden to protect the first humans. Alas, security was not tight enough to save the first couple.

**An Angel brings nourishment to the Hebrew prophet Elijah. (Gustave Dore illustration)**

**Uzza**. In ancient Jewish folklore, Uzza vies with Rahab (See Rahab) for the dishonor of being the guardian angel of Egypt. In one legend cited by scholar Bernard J. Bamberger, a trial of sorts is going on in heaven. Uzza argues like a defense lawyer before an angelic jury, defending his clients on earth, the Egyptians. He says that the Egyptian army pursuing the Jews across the Red Sea should be spared drowning by God. Uzza's plea for clemency (capital punishment, he said, was excessive for merely enslaving a people) was foiled, however. What turned the verdict against Pharaoh was this: The archangel Gabriel suddenly introduced as evidence a brick which cruel Egyptian taskmasters had forced an Israelite slave to make for one of Pharaoh's building projects.

**Valkyries**. (Choosers of the Slain) In Viking folklore, these horse-mounted maiden goddesses acted like "angels of death," escorting newly dead warriors into the afterlife. Their flashing armor caused the Northern Lights as they zipped over battlefields, choosing which of the barbarians should be killed in the fighting. Then, the valkyries scooped up the dead warriors' spirits and hauled them up to head god Odin's beer hall in the clouds, *Valhalla*. As they did so, they crossed over the rainbow bridge connecting heaven and earth. After the newly-dead fighters alit in Odin's barbarian paradise, the warriors spent all night wenching, feasting and swilling ale. At dawn, the heavenly warriors began fighting each other for fun, cut themselves completely to bloody pieces by sunset, were then resurrected from death by Odin to start a new cycle of gorging and womanizing by night and bloodletting by day.

**Victor**. Of course, St. Patrick gets the credit for spearheading the Christianization of Ireland, but according to legend, the angel Victor was behind it all. Victor supposedly appeared before St. Patrick during the twilight years of the Roman Empire and asked Patrick go back to an Ireland he had escaped from. Here's what had happened: At age 16, Patrick, had been kidnapped from a well-to-do Christian family in Roman Britain and had ended up as a slave tending swine in Ireland. But a supernatural voice eventually gave Patrick detailed directions for an escape to the south of Ireland, where a ship was to take him to what is now France. Later, though, legend says Victor made his request to Patrick to return to Ireland, and history was changed when Patrick heeded it.

**Virtues**. The fifth-highest of the nine orders of angels in the Catholic Church's traditional belief. They draw on God's force to work miracles on earth. They also cooperate with the order of powers to keep the physical laws of the universe working. And the virtues steel the nerve of good people whose noble goals face tough challenges. (See Pseudo-Dionysius)

**Vision Quest**. This was one of the most important events in the lives of many Indians. The "vision quest" was an Indian's trek into the wilderness in an attempt to get a guardian spirit to appear and to stay with him permanently.

At puberty, a young Indian would often go out naked into a sacred place in the wilds to endure ordeals until this spirit appeared. By fasting, meditating -- in exceptional cases even practicing self-mutilation, among other things -- the Indian greatly stressed the mind and body until "otherworldly" visions began -- a technique often used by mystics. The Indian might go into a trance or have a dream in which the guardian spirit appears, generally looking like an animal. The brave then asks the spirit's help in everyday matters of living. Sometimes, however, the vision quest is not aimed at getting a guardian spirit but simply at receiving advice from the Great Spirit or spirit world in general.

**Vohu Manah**. Legend gives credit to this archangel for starting up the onetime major religion of Zoroastrianism -- a religion that radically changed Judaism's beliefs and so indirectly heavily influenced Christian doctrines. Vohu Manah (Good Mind) is the messenger archangel who revealed God's Word to the prophet Zoroaster around 600 B.C., according to Zoroastrians. (Like Gabriel's revelation to Mohammed.) Zoroaster then went on to found Zoroastrianism, which became the religion of the huge ancient Persian Empire. Later, Zoroastrianism greatly influenced Judaism, and indirectly, Christianity -- by introducing new ideas of heaven and hell, good and bad angels fighting each other, a Last Judgment and Final Resurrection, etc. Zoroaster taught that Ahura Mazda (The Lord Wisdom), who was the Principle of Goodness, was constantly at war with his co-equal twin brother Angra Mainyu (Fiendish Spirit), who was the Principle of Evil.

**Voices**. A whole class of angel intervention stories exists in which persons claim that an angel or some other invisible being has spoken to them telepathically.

Some people, like Socrates, claim that they get continual advice. But in most cases, the incidents are isolated and serve to warn the person of danger or of somebody's need. Here are a few stories told to me over the years:

■ An Alabama technician told me in an interview that he was in a chicken house on a winter's day with his small son. Suddenly, he said, he heard an urgent mental voice say to him: "Get out!" Reacting in a stimulus-response way, he instantly grabbed the boy and ran out of the building -- just before it collapsed under the weight of heavy ice on the roof.

■ At a talk show I was on, a woman caller offered this story: She said she was driving past a strange house when a voice out of nowhere told her to stop and pull in at the residence. Unable to resist this urging, she did so against her better judgment. When she came to the door, a desperate woman opened it and pleaded for help: Her husband had just suffered a grave medical crisis.

**War in Heaven**. In Christian legend, this was the great battle fought at the dawn of time between good angels, supporting God's rule over the universe, and the rebelling bad angels, supporting Satan's attempt to take God's place. Actually, the Old Testament says nothing about any war in heaven or fallen angels.

In literature, perhaps the most exciting imaginative story is in the blind Puritan poet John Milton's multi-volume *Paradise Lost*. Here, an arrogant Satan leads rebelling angels against faithful ones defending the Mount of God in heaven as mountains are ripped up and tossed around like cannonballs. Although the bad angels feel pain and the good ones don't, the forces are evenly matched until the Son (Jesus Christ not yet born on earth as a man) takes the field. The Son terrifies Lucifer's army by hurling thunderbolts. Heaven's crystal wall opens up to reveal a "bottomless" pit into which the panicky rebels throw themselves. Lucifer and his plummeting angels crash land in hell and end up chained by a burning lake of fire. Eventually freeing themselves, the rebels and their dictator Lucifer, his face scarred by the Son's thunder, build hell's capital city, Pandemonium ("All-Demon") At Lucifer's instigation, hell's rubber-stamp parliament formally declares war. Meanwhile, God sends his Son to create the world in six days, including Adam and Eve. However, Satan eventually corrupts the first humans to revenge himself against God, yet accomplishes nothing. As he returns to hell to gloat, God turns him and his fellow devils into hissing serpents.

Some Middle Ages philosophers, in their airy debates about the who, what, where, when and why of the War in Heaven, concluded that the conflict lasted three seconds and that Lucifer and certain devils fell to hell while others stayed in the earth's air to tempt mankind.

Some extremely creative commentators have even speculated that heaven's great battle took place on a planet in the solar system which exploded and gave rise to the asteroid belt between Mars and Jupiter!

**Weyer, Johann**. During the 1500s and 1600s, early modern writers developed an elaborate mythology of hell and its pecking order, complete with infernal bureaucrats and even fiendish ambassadors to earthly nations. Johann Weyer came up with one of the most complicated organizations. Counting pitchforks, Weyer claimed that hell has 7,405,926 devils in 1,111 divisions under 72 princes. But certain Lutherans later decided that the true number of devils was actually exactly 2,665,866,746,664, or, very roughly, 2.6 trillion.

**Wings of Angels**. The early books of the Old Testament say nothing about their angels having wings. Also, the earliest Christian artists showed angels as wingless youths. In fact, angel wings did not start to crop up in Christian art until roughly the era of Rome's first Christian emperor, Constantine, in the 300s A.D. Then, angels often began to take on the winged look of the Greek goddess of victory, Nike. In reality, spiritual beings that flit about with the speed of thought probably don't need literal wings. Still, wings are good symbols of that "rapid flight." Nevertheless, for those who have to figure out everything, consider this thought from J.B.S. Haldane: "An angel whose muscles developed no more power weight for weight than those of an eagle or a pigeon would require a breast projecting for about four feet to house the muscles engaged in working its wings, while to economize in weight, its legs would have to be reduced to mere stilts."

**Wormwood**. An indirectly named angel, called a "star" in the Bible's Book of Revelation, who played a role in the earth's torments during the end times. In Revelation, the visionary John of (the Greek Aegean island) Patmos has a vision of the end of the world. He sees God on his throne, holding a momentous book fastened shut with seven seals. No one on earth can open the book except a seven-eyed and seven-horned Lamb (Christ), who systematically breaks the book's seals -- each time releasing a disaster for the earth or some wonder. The first four opened seals release the Four Horsemen of the Apocalypse. The horseman War is riding a red horse, Famine a black one, death a pale horse, and Civil Conflict a white horse -- symbols of the world's woes, then and now. The breaking of the fifth seal touched off a vision of martyrs who cried out for justice against their assassins. The tearing of the sixth seal caused the sun to become black, the moon blood-red, and the earth to quake savagely. Following the rupture of the seventh and last seal, amid other torments, a large flaming "star" (an angel) called Wormwood (Bitterness) streaked down to earth, landing on a third of the earth's rivers and springs, poisoning them and causing many mortal deaths.

**Yazatas.** In the former world religion of Zoroastrianism, the yazatas are lesser angels who watch over the tiniest of details: There are even Yazatas who look after the individual hours and minutes of the day. Among the more famous yazatas is the 10,000-eyed sun warrior Mithra, a champion of truth who later became a god in his own religion and whose birthday was chosen by Christian leaders to be the date for Christmas. (See Mithra) Another notable yazata is Sraosha, the all-hearing angel who listens for mortals complaining about evil done to them. Sraosha helps Mithra and the angel Rashnu judge the souls of the dead according to their good and bad deeds. The Yazatas take their orders from archangels called *Holy Immortals*.

**Zadkiel**. (The Righteousness of God) Some believe it was Zadkiel (Others say Michael) who stopped Abraham from killing his young son as a sacrifice to God. As a result, Zadkiel's symbol is a sacrificial knife.

**Zagzagel**. (Divine Splendor) The angel who tutored Moses. Zagzagel is also a linguist with a repertoire of 70 languages, according to Jewish legend. When it was Moses' time to die, Zagzagel helped the archangels Michael and Gabriel take Moses from earth to heaven after the Lawgiver had chased away the angel of death, Samael, beating him blind with his fabled staff.

**Zephon**. In apocryphal books, Zephon was a would-be heavenly arsonist. The story began when Lucifer talked the brilliant angel Zephon into defecting to the dark side during the War in Heaven. Zephon immediately turned his genius to hatching a plan for setting heaven on fire. But the devils lost the celestial war and were thrown down to hell before Zephon's plan could be carried out. Zephon must now, appropriately, forever beat his wings to continually fan the embers of hell.

# Books on Angels & Related Topics

■ Adler, Mortimer. *The Angels and Us*. Macmillan Publishing Co., N.Y. 1982. The famed philosopher provides a well-synthesized summary of centuries of philosophical thinking about angels.

■ Anderson, Joan Wester. *Where Angels Walk*. Barton & Brett, Publishers. Sea Cliff, New York. 1992. A series of compelling stories of particularly dramatic encounters between humans and angels. Warm and inspirational reading.

■ Begbie, Harold. *On the Side of the Angels: A Reply to Arthur Machen*. Hodder and Stoughton, London. 1915. A detailed account of the alleged sightings of saints and angels on the western battlefront of Europe during World War I.

■ Blackmore, Rev. Simon. *The Angel World*. John Winterich, Cleveland. 1927.

■ Boros, Ladislaus. *Angels and Men*. Seabury Press, N.Y. 1977.

■ Brewer, Rev. Cobham. *A Dictionary of Miracles*. Gale Research Co., Detroit. 1966. A detailed survey of miracle lore regarding saints, angels and the like, much of it from the Middle Ages.

■ Burnham, Sophy. *A Book of Angels*. Ballantine Books, New York. 1990. A very personal and sensitive book with a beautiful gold foil cover that soared onto the bestseller lists. Many interesting stories and facts.

■ --------. *Angel Letters*. Ballantine Books, New York. 1991. The popular sequel to *A Book of Angels*, which inspired many readers to write letters to Ms. Burnham about their own angelic experiences. This is a collection of those letters, with stories told in the writers' own words.

■ Cameron, Ann. *The Angel Book*. Ballantine Books, N.Y. 1977. One of the better general surveys of the angel world.

■ Church, F. Forrester. *Entertaining Angels*. Harper & Row, San Francisco. 1987. A witty and light-hearted look at the world of angels from the eyes of a religious progressive.

■ Clement, Clara. *Angels in Art*. L.C. Page & Co., Boston. 1898.

■ Danielou, Jean. *The Angels and Their Mission*. The Newman Press, Westminster, Maryland.

■ Davidson, Gustav. *A Dictionary of Angels*. The Free Press, New York. 1971. A browser's delight for more than two decades. Davidson, the author-editor of a dozen books, spent 15 years researching this 414-page classic. Unsurpassed for angel scholarship (the bibliography covers 25 pages of small type!), this highly recommended volume may be the most detailed and scholarly look at angel folklore and legend in existence.

■ Field. *Angels and Ministers of Grace*. Hill and Wang, N.Y. 1971.

■ Fowler, Alfred. *Our Angels Friends in Ministry and Song*. (No publisher listed)

■ Freeman, Eileen. *Touched by Angels*. (Scheduled for publication in August 1993 by Warner Books, New York) Eileen Freeman burst onto the national scene in 1992 -- the "year of the angel," when national media reported on a resurgence of interest in angels that had been building momentum for some time. As editor of AngelWatch newsletter, a periodical reporting hard news and features about angels, Freeman found herself repeatedly behind microphones and in front of TV cameras. Here, she tells how angels personally have touched her life and those of others.

■ Gaebelain, Arno. *The Angels of God*. Our Hope Publication Office, N.Y. 1924.

■ Gilmore, Don. *Angels, Angels Everywhere*. Pilgrim, N.Y. 1981.

■ Godwin, Malcolm. *Angels: An Endangered Species*. Simon and Shuster, New York. 1990. This large and attractive hardcover book for the coffee table has almost 200 gorgeous illustrations, most of them in color. Fine coverage of angel folklore, spiced with Godwin's wit and whimsy.

■ Goldman, Karen. *The Angel Book*. Simon and Shuster, New York. 1992. An inspirational series of beautiful short thoughts and proverbs on things angelic.

■ Graham, Billy. *Angels: God's Secret Agents*. Pocket Books, N.Y. 1975. The famous evangelist's best-seller presents evangelical Christian opinion about angels. Interlaced with anecdotes.

■ Hahn, Emily. *Breaths of God*. Doubleday & Co., New York. 1971. A sweet and whimsical look at the world of angels, written with a light touch.

■ Hall, Manley. *The Blessed Angels*. The Philosophical Research Society, Los Angeles. 1980.

Harrison, Margaret. *Angels Then and Now* Branch-Smith, Fort Worth. 1975.

■ Howard, Jane. *Commune with the Angels*. A.R.E. Press, Virginia Beach, Va. 1992. The author presents her system for developing an awareness of the angelic presence.

■ Humann, Harvey. *The Many Faces of Angels*. DeVorss & Co., Publisher, Marina del Rey, Calif. 1986. A thought-provoking basic introduction to the world of angels with many fresh, unconventional ideas on the subject.

■ Jameson, Anna. *Legends of the Madonna*. Longmans, Green and Co., London. 1890.

■ Joppie, A.S. *The Ministry of Angels*. Baker Book House. Grand Rapids, Mich. 1953.

■ Latham, Henry. *A Service of Angels*. Deighton, Bell & Co., Cambridge. 1896.

■ Leadbeater, C.W. *Invisible Helpers*. Theosophical Publishing Concern, Chicago. 1915. Presents the viewpoint that departed human souls, acting like ministering angels, are actively helping rescue, comfort and otherwise minister to us. Contains interesting anecdotes.

■ Leaveil, Landrum. *Angels, Angels, Angels*. Broadman Press, Nashville. 1973.

■ Lloyd, Marjorie Lewis. *It Must Have Been an Angel*. Pacific Press Publishing Association, Mountain View, Calif. 1980.

■ Lockyer, Herbert. *The Mystery and Ministry of Angels*. Eerdmans Publishing Co., Grand Rapids, Mich. 1958.

■ MacGregor, Geddes. *Angels: Ministers of Grace*. Paragon House, New York. 1988. The prominent theologian Geddes MacGregor's interesting discussion of angels in art, literature, music, mythology, and the Bible. Among the interesting subjects covered: the possibility that humans may evolve into angels.

■ McConkie, Oscar, Jr. *Angels*. Deseret Book Co., Salt Lake City, Utah. 1975. A discussion of angels from the Mormon perspective.

■ Miller, Leslie Miller. *All About Angels*. Regal Books, Glendale, Calif. 1976.

■ Moody, Raymond, Jr. *Life After Life*. Bantam Books, N.Y. A psychiatrist, Moody collected, offhand for years, scores of personal anecdotes of near-death experiences. In this landmark book, which classified the stages of near-death experiences, Moody notes that near-death survivors often claim to have met brilliant "beings of light." These angel-like entities were prepared to escort them to the Beyond or turn them back to the living.

■ ---------. *Reflections on Life After Life*. Bantam Books, N.Y. 1978. The sequel to *Life After Life* in which Moody describes how persons brushing with death claim to have glimpsed happy "cities of light."

- Moolenburgh, Hans. *A Handbook of Angels*. C.W. Daniel Co., Saffron Walden, England. 1984. A wide-ranging and lively discussion by a Dutch surgeon who made headlines in Holland in connection with angels. Moolenburgh conducted an informal survey of 400 of his patients to see how frequently ordinary people see angels. Eight per cent claimed to have had the experience.
- --------. *Meetings With Angels*. C.W. Daniel Co., Saffron Walden, England. 1992. 101 angel encounter stories, based on letters written to the author in response to *A Handbook of Angels*.
- Morse, Melvin and Paul Perry. *Closer to the Light*. Ballantine Books, New York. 1990. A pediatrician's touching investigation of the near-death experiences of children he interviewed. This popular book is based on a study which was published in the pediatric journal of the AMA.
- Mould, Daphne. *Angels of God*. Devin-Adair Co., N.Y. 1963.
- Newhouse, Flower. *Natives of Eternity*. J.F. Rowny Press, Santa Barbara, Calif. 1937. A theosophical clairvoyant describes her visions of the angel world.
- O'Sullivan, Paul. *All About the Angels*. A well-written pocket-sized book in the Roman Catholic tradition. Tan Books, Rockford, Ill. 1990.
- Palmer, Tobias. *An Angel in my House*. Ave Maria Press, Notre Dame, Ind. 1975.
- Parente, Alessio. *Send Me Your Guardian Angel*. Editions Carlo Tozza Napoli. 1984. Recounts the life of the famous Catholic priest Padre Pio, who told those requesting his help to send him their guardian angel if they could not come themselves.
- Parente, Pascal. *Beyond Space*. Tan Books, Rockford, Ill. 1973. A popularly written Roman Catholic exposition of angels by a leading theologian and priest.
- Parisen, Maria (Compiler). *Angels and Mortals*. Theosophical Publishing House. Wheaton, Ill. 1990. A collection of mostly metaphysically oriented articles by prominent authors. Topics include the mystic Emanuel Swedenborg's reports of angel encounters, the native American holy man Black Elk's visionary ascent to heaven, Mohammed's vision of Gabriel, etc.
- Paula, Mary. *Presenting the Angels*. Benziger Brothers. 1935.

■ Regamy, Raymond. *What is an Angel?* Hawthorn Books, N.Y. 1960.

■ Richards, H.M.S., Jr. *Angels – Secret Agents of God and Satan.* Review and Herald Publishing Association, Nashville. 1980.

■ Ring, Kenneth. *Life at Death.* Coward, McCann and Geoghegan, N.Y. After Raymond Moody's pioneering classification of the stages of the near-death experience (NDE), Ring and others conducted scientific investigations of the NDE phenomenon.

■ Ronner, John. *Do You Have a Guardian Angel?* Mamre Press, Murfreesboro, Tenn. 1985. Journalist Ronner spent 14 months researching the subject of angels for this newspaper-style book, organized in question and answer form.

■ Sabom, Michael. *Recollections of Death: A Medical Investigation.* Harper & Row, N.Y. 1982. Sabom conducted one of several scientifically oriented studies of the near-death experience.

■ *St. Michael and the Angels.* Tan Books and Publishers, Rockford, Ill. 1983.

■ Taylor, Terry Lynn. *Messengers of Light.* H.J. Kramer, Tiburon, Calif. 1990. Taylor's positive and upbeat best-seller combines angels and self-help.

■ --------. *Guardians of Hope.* H.J. Kramer, Tiburon, Calif. Taylor's sequel to *Messengers of Light* and its concepts.

■ --------. *Answers From the Angels.* H.J. Kramer, Tiburon, Calif. 1993. Taylor received thousands of letters from readers of *Messengers of Light*, much of the mail describing correspondents' experiences with angels. This is a selection from the mailbag, with stories told in the writer's own words.

■ Ward, Theodora. *Men and Angels.* Viking Press, N.Y. 1969. A well-written general survey of the angel world, with several glossy sections of illustrations by classic artists.

■ Westermann, Claus. *God's Angels Need No Wings.* Fortress Press. 1979.

■ Wilson, Peter. *Angels.* Pantheon Books, N.Y. 1980. A nicely illustrated coffee table book. Wilson does a particularly good job of crossing cultures as he examines angelology. He is especially informative about Muslim lore concerning angels.

# Index

**A**
Abdiel, 8
Abou Ben Adhem, 123
Abraham, 31
    & three angels, 8
    Zadkiel, 171, 161
    in Eden, 148
Acts of the Holy Angels, 9
Adam, 34
    and Lilith, 93
    and Samael, 139
    Book of Angel Raziel, 134
    goes to Mecca, 85
    Iblis won't bow, 85
    in Paradise Lost, 62
    in Zoroastrianism, 69
    jealous demiurge, 56
    magic skins, 116
    on deathbed, 105
    sees Dante, 51
    sees Raphael, 132
Aeons, 9, 150
Aesthma, 151
Af, 11
Ahriman, 11, 27
    birth of, 69
Ahura Mazda, 11, 69, 152
    Holy Immortals, 84
Al Arat, 12
Albertus Magnus, 28
Allah
    banishes Iblis, 85
    creates man, 34
    punishes Hawwa, 85
    stops Israfil's tears, 87

Allen, Richard, 48
Amesha Spentas, 83
Anderson, Joan Wester, 14
Androgyns, 73
Ange passe, 69
Angel authors, 13, 121
    Begbie, Harold, 22, 38
    Burnham, Sophy, 13
    Church, Forrester, 80
    Davidson, Gustav, 53
    Clement, Clara, 32
    Freeman, Eileen, 14
    Godwin, Malcolm, 38
    Graham, Billy, 14
    Hodson, Geoffrey, 40
    Howard, Jane, 14
    Jung, Leo, 150
    MacGregor, Geddes, 29
    Moolenburgh, Hans, 36
    Ronner, John, 14
    Taylor, Terry, 14
    Wilson, Peter, 120
Angel books, 136
Angel Collectors Club of America, 14
Angel holidays, 15
    guardian angels, 15, 77
    feast of Uriel, 15
    Portugal guardian 66
    Michaelmas, 15, 105
Angel of Death, 16
    Assyrian army, 53
    as Af
    as Samael, 139
    Azrael, 34

latin superstition, 157
valkyries, 164
Angel of Peace, 18
Angel of the Furnace, 17
Angel of the Lord, 18
Angel orgs, 14, 26, 121
Angel wrapped in cloud, 18
Angelic encounters, 63, 123
Angelolatry, 18
Angelology, 19
Angelophany, 19
Angelos, 19
Angels
    and judgment, 30
    androgyns, 73
    at Christ's tomb, 41
    art, 30
    belief in, 38, 124
    crackdown on, 86
    dancing on pin, 129
    disguised as mortals, 21
    earliest depiction, 31
    foreign sayings, 68
    frequency in Bible, 41
    gender, 73
    ghosts, 74
    guardian spirit, 12
    higher self, 13
    in the Bible, 24, 41, 52-54, 103, 113, 120, 146
    intuition, 153-54
    language of, 15
    life span of, 93
    marriage, 73
    movies, 46, 109-110
    named in Bible, 143
    named in the Koran, 143
    neglect by, 113-14

number of, 67, 125
origin of, 12
over nations, 65
root of word, 19
physical intervention, 121, 124, 160-161
population explosion, 86, 152
races of, 156
renewed interest, 134-35
saints, 138
sealed in grace?, 68
sex with humans, 33, 66
sports, 77
stamps, 126
stars, 48
strict definition of, 12
superior being, 12
traffic, 77, 159-161
veneration of, 18
warfare, 22, 35
wings, 116
Angels Can Fly, 21
Angels of Mons, 22-24
    Arthur Machen, 24
Angels of Terror
    debate Moses, 79
Angels of the World, 26
Angels of Truth & Peace, 26
AngelWatch newsletter, 26
Angra Mainyu, 27
Anpiel, 27
Anthroposophical Soc., 152
Apocalypse of Abraham, 19
Apocalypse of St. Peter, 162
Apollyon, 27
Apsara, 28
Aquinas, Thomas, 28, 43, 154, 156
    and illumination, 16
    angel bodies, 42

Arabic
    tongue of Djibril, 16
Archangels, 29
    Gabriel, 71
    Holy Immortals, 83-4
    in art, 31
    Michael, 103
    Raphael, 132
    Sariel, 143
    7 archangels, 146
    Vohu Manah, 166
    Zoroastrian, 11
Archons, 56
Armageddon (see End times)
Art and angels, 30
    Acts of the Holy Angels, 9
    Gabriel, 72
    glory of angels, 75
    Mary, 98
    Nike, 116
Ashmedai, 32
Asmodeus, 33, 132
Assyrian Empire, 53
Augustine, 154
Aura, 80
Authors, 13
Avesta, 11
Avicenna, 83
Azazel, 33, 145, 148
Azrael, 16, 34

**B**

Baalpeor, 40
Babylonian Captivity, 17, 97
Bailey, George, 46
Balaam, 41
Balberith, 35
Baradiel, 152
Bardiel, 65

Barrett, William, 55
Battle of the Bulge, 36
Bayless, Raymond, 64, 81
Beatrice, 51
Beelzebub, 36
    Lord of the Flies, 38
Begbie, Harold
    belief in angels, 38
Being of Light,
    description of, 111
Belief in angels, polls, 124
Beliel, 40
Belphegor, 40
    surveys marriage, 40
Beth-el, 88
Bethelda, 40
Bishops Wife, The, 109
Blake, William, 31
    angels' holiness, 131
Bodhisattva, 41
Bodies of angels, 42
    quodlibet, 129
Book of Adam, 139
Book of Adam & Eve, 89, 104
Book of Daniel
    fiery furnace, 17
Book of Enoch, 115, 147, 152
Book of Jubilees, 99
Book of Mormon, 108
Book of Revelation, 170
    and Apollyon, 27
    angel in cloud, 18
    fallen angels, 67
    Wormwood, 170
Book of the Angel Raziel, 134
Book of Tobit
    and Asmodeus, 33
Brahma & the Buddha, 98
Bridge of Discrimination, 11
Brutus, Cassius & Judas
    Satan chews, 142

Buddha
    and Mara, 97
    and Brahma, 98
Buddhism
    bodhisattvas, 41
Bulbuka, Grace, 112
Buraq
    carrying Mohammed, 59
Burnham, Sophy, 13

**C**
Cain, 16, 105
Cardinal of Tusculum, 67
Chain of being, 43
Chamuel, 43
Cherubim, 45, 127
    evolution of, 45
    posted at Eden, 41
Cherubs, 128
Chesterton, Gilbert, 129
Children, 43
    Bulbuka story, 112
    seeing angels, 44
Christ, 141
    children's angels, 77
    Doomsday book, 170
    helped by Chamuel, 43
    in Gnosticism, 151
    in Islam, 87
    in War in Heaven, 168
    marriage & angels, 73
    meets Mohammed, 59
    Nazareth house, 126
    quote on children, 44
    storms hell, 36, 94
    tempted by Satan, 97
    vs. Ialdabaoth, 56
Christianity
    and angel art, 30
    built on Judaism, 12, 166
Christmas
    setting date, 106
Church, F. Forrester, 80, 131
Cinvat Bridge, 133
Circumcision & Moses, 11
Clarence, 46
Clark, William E., 160
Clement, Clara, 32
Cocytus, 50
Coincidence & angels, 13, 46, 47
Comfort from angels
    Paul Swope, 78
Conception & Lailah, 92
Conductor of souls, 16, 103
Conferences of angels, 47
Constantine, 116
Constellations, 48
    Kakabel, 91
Contact with the dead
    Andrew Greeley survey, 125
Cowper, William
    suicide foiled, 47
Crackdown on angels
    by Church council, 86
Creation of angels, 49
    Davidson quote, 130
    Israfil's breath, 87
Creation of humankind
    and Azrael, 34
    angels of truth and peace object, 26
    Iblis banished, 84

Shemhazai, Azazel, 148
Creation of the world
and Rahab, 131
Cush, 116

**D**
Daimon, 19
and Socrates, 52, 151
description of, 52
Daniel, 61
and Gabriel, 71
Dante, 49, 122
visits afterlife, 49, 50-51
Dark Angel, 52-53
as Chamuel, 43
Davidson, Gustav
angel encounter, 53
on angels, 130
Day of Atonement, 34
Deathbed visions, 17, 54-55
Jennie & Edith, 55
Demiurge, 55
Devil
in Buddhism, 97
in Gnosticism, 151
in Islam, 84
Devils
came from giants, 58
number of, 169
Dickens, Charles, 158
Dickinson, Emily, 123
Dionysius, 127
Disraeli, Benjamin, 130
Divine Comedy, 142
Divine spark, 10
Djibril, 59
Djinn, 147
Doomsday (See End times)

Draco, 48
Dubbiel, 60, 66
replaces Gabriel, 60
Duerer, Albrecht, 31
Duns Scotus
angel bodies, 42

**E**
Eckhart, Meister, 130
Eden, 61
Egypt, on trial, 164
Elijah, 153
is Sandalphon, 141
Elisha & Assyrian army, 35
Emerson, Ralph Waldo, 114
Encounters with angels
frequency of, 123
End of the world (See End times)
End times
Christ opens book, 170
Gabriel's trumpet, 71
in Zoroastrianism, 12, 69-70
Israfil, 87
John of Patmos, 169-70
Michael, 104
Wormwood, 169-70
Enoch, 103, 147
angel of peace, 18
is Metatron, 102
Book of Raziel, 134
Enochian angels, 65, 68, 91, 144
Penemue, 119
Raguel, 131
Remiel, 134
Epistle to Hebrews, 8
Erelim
over plants, 64
Ethiopic Book of Enoch, 64

Ethnarchs, 65, 117
  struggle in heaven, 60
Evil, problem of, 89
Ezekiel, 96, 159

**F**
Fallen angels, 147
  ethnarchs corrupted, 65
  Harut & Marut, 82
  mating with mortals, 68, 115, 144
  number of, 82
  origin of, 66-67
  replaced by humans? 67
  Satan won't bow to Adam, 104
  seen by Enoch, 103
  Shemhazai, Azazel, 149
  Sophia, 150-51
Faust, 100-101
Final Judgment, 150
  in Zoroastrianism, 170
Final Trumpet
  Israfil blows, 87
  Horn Blows at Midnight, The, 110
Fioretti, 68
First Book of Adam & Eve, 62
Five ages of man, 75
Fletcher, John, 130
Flood, 58, 148
  wipes out giants, 145
Fodor, Nandor, 158
Food of angels, 97
Forbidden Knowledge, 33, 68
Forever Darling, 109

Four Horsemen, 171
Fra Angelico, 31
Frashkart, 12, 69
Fravashi, 70

**G**
Gershom, 11
Gibbor, 48, 100, 115, 145, 148
Giotti, 32
Glory of angels, 75
Gnosticism
  and aeons, 9
  & demiurge, 55
  Sophia, 151
God
  Gnosticism, 10, 151
  kisses Moses, 139
  passes Elijah, 153
  quizzed by Abraham, 89
Godwin, Malcolm, 38, 114
Goethe, Johann von, 101
Golden age of man, 75
Gospel of Nicodemus, 36
Graham, Billy, 13
Great Spirit, 166
Greeley, Andrew, 125
Gregory the Great, 67, 156
Grey, Margot, 82
Guardian angels
  11,000 for each, 76
  and Padre Pio, 117
  daimon, 52
  fravashi, 70
  number, 76
  thought-forms, 157-8
Guardian spirit, 12, 77-78
  daimon warns Socrates, 150
  fylgir, 70

genius, 74
golden race, 75
in film, 109
Juno, 74
Lares, 93
Pen-Ming, 120
spirit guide, 151
vision quest, 165-66
widows & widowers, 13

**H**
Ha-satan, 142-43
Hadarniel, 78-79
Hades, 149
Hafaza, 79
Haldane, J.B.S., 169
Halo, 30, 79-80, 98
Halo Everybody! 15
Hamlet, 130
Harps, 81
Harut & Marut, 82
Hawwa, 85
Hayy, 83
Healing at Lourdes, 99
Heaven
    Abraham, 88
    fundamentalists, 80
    arson try, 171
    as Nirvana, 117
    Dante visits, 51
    Enoch, 102
    Mohammed ascends, 59
    Moses ascends, 78, 91
    music, 81, 123
    quartermaster of, 161
    seven heavens, 146
    Swedenborg, 157

Visited by fundamentalists, 80
    War in, 167-68
Heaven Can Wait, 110
Hebrew
    tongue of angels, 15
    universal tongue, 117
Helen of Troy
    and Faust, 101
Hell
    & Malik, 95
    & Moses, 111, 153
    djahannam, 59
    in Judaism, 73, 150
    infernal empire, 58, 169
    Swedenborg, 157
    seen by Dante, 50
Here Comes Mr. Jordan, 110
Hermes, 83, 153
Hermesiel, 83, 153
heywood, Thomas, 127
Hezekiah, 53
Hierarchy of angels
    archangels, 29
    cherubim, 45
    Dionysius, 127
    dominions, 60
    powers, 127
    princes, 127
    rank confusion, 29
    seraphim, 127, 145
    Steiner, Rudolf, 152
    thrones, 159
    virtues, 165
Higher self, 13, 112
Highway to Heaven, 90
Hill, Napoleon
    imaginary council, 158
Hiva and Hiyya, 148
Hodson, Geoffrey, 40

Horatio, 130
Horn Blows at Midnight, 109
Howard, Jane, 14
Hundred Years' War, 104
Hunt, Leigh, 123
Huris, 84

**I**
Ialdabaoth, as Yahweh, 56
Iblis, 82, 84
 chief of Jinn, 89
 Mohammed teaches
 great-grandson, 147
Incubi, 58
Indians
 vision quest, 165
Indra, 28
Infernal ambassadors
 Hutjin to Italy, 114
 M a m m o n t o
 England, 95
 Thamuz to Spain,
 114
Infernal Empire, 58, 168
Iniaes
 church condemns,
 85
Intellect of angels, 86
Interest in angels, 134-35
Intuition, 153-54
Isa, 87
 meets Mohammed,
 59
Isaiah, 127
Iscariot, Judas
 Satan chews, 142
Ishtar, 148
Islam
 al Arat, 12
 angel art, 30
 hafaza, 79

 shaitans, 147
Islamic angels
 Azrael, 34
 Djibril, 59
 Israfil, 87
 Malik, 95
 Mikal, 105
 Munkar & Nakir, 110
 Ridwan, 137
Israel
 Michael as national
 guardian of, 103
Israfil, 87
It's a Wonderful Life, 46
Ithuriel, 88
 searches for Satan, 88
It's a Wonderful Life, 109

**J**
Jacob
 Dark Angel, 52-53
Jacob's Ladder, 88
 climbed by Dante, 51
Jaoel, 88-89
Jinn, 89
Joan of Arc, 104
 observed in World War I,
 22
Joel, 89
John of Patmos
 end times vision, 169
 angel in cloud, 18
Johnson, Ben, 124
Jophiel, 91
Judaism
 angel art in, 30
 hell and purgatory, 73
 kabbalah, 144
 sheol, 149
 Zoroastrian influence
 on, 143, 166

Judgment
    by Michael, 104
    by Minos, 106
    by Rashnu, 133
Jung, Leo, 149
Juno, 74

**K**
Ka, 91
Kabbalah, 144
Kabbalistic angels, 144
    Anpiel, 27
    Mehiel, 100
    Metatron, 102
    Pahaliah, 119
Kakabel, 91
Karma, 114
Keller, Helen, 157
Kemuel
    and Moses, 91
King David
    pestilence angel, 120
    freed from hell, 38
Kokabiel, 65
Koran, 59
Koranic angels, 143

**L**
Lahash: Moses prayer, 92
Lailah, 92
Landon, Michael, 90
Language of angels, 15
Lares, 93
Last Judgment (see Judgment)
Latin, tongue of angels, 16
Law of Compensation, 114
Leliel, 65
Life After Life, 112
Life review
    during NDE, 112

    Swedenborg, 157
Life span of angels, 93
Lilim, 93
Lilith, 93
Limbo
    in Catholicism, 94
    in Islam, 12
    seen by Dante, 50
Lithuania angel stamp, 126
Locke, John, 43
London Evening News, 24
Lord Byron, 123
Los Angeles
    origin of name, 99
Lourdes, 99

**M**
MacGregor, Geddes, 29
Machen, Arthur, 24
Madonna, and Michael, 104
Malaika, 94
Malakh, 19
Malik, 59, 95
Mammon, 95
Man Clothed in Linen, 96
Manna, 97, 146
Mara, 97
Marian visions, 99
Marriage, and angels, 73
Mary, 98
Mashya and Mashyoi, 69
Mastema, 99-100
Mather, Increase, 14
Matriel, 65
Mefathiel, 100
Mehiel, 100
Mephistopheles, 100-101
Merkabah rider, 101
Metatron, 102-103, 146, 149
    carries prayer, 141

Michael, 103-105, 146, 153, 158
    as angel of death, 16
    feast day, 15
    & fallen angels, 145
    Israel's angel, 65
    in World War I, 22
Michaelangelo
    & Fra Angelica, 31
Michaelmas, 15, 105
Mikal, 105
Milton, John, 106
Miltonian angels
    Abdiel, 8
    Ithuriel, Xaphan, 88
    Mulciber, 110
    Thammuz, 106
    Uriel, 162
Minos, 50, 106
Mithra, 106-107, 171
Mithras, 107
Mohammed
    sees Gabriel, 59, 71
    teaches jinn, 147
Mons, Belgium, angels of, 22
Moody, Raymond, 111-112
Moolenburgh, Hans, 36, 135
    coincidence, 47
    survey by, 124
Moore, Carole, 44
Mormon angels, 108
Moroni, 108
Morse, Melvin, 45
Moses
    Af swallows, 11
    & Hadarniel, 78
    and Kemuel, 91
    beats Samael, 139
    Lahash, 92
    Rahab opposes, 131
    tours Eden, 148

    visits hell, 111, 153
    Zagzagel tutors, 171
Movie Angels, 109-110
    Clarence, 46
Mulciber, 110
Munkar & Nakir, 110
Music and angels
    Jaoel, choir leader
Music in heaven, 81, 123

**N**
Nad, 81
Nasargiel, 111, 153
National angels, 65, 116
    Michael, 103
National Opinion Research Center, 125
Nazi blitzkrieg in Holland in 1940, 124
Near-death experience, 17, 111-112
    and angel bodies, 42
    OBE experience, 111
    polls, 125
Nebuchadnezzer, 17, 61, 96
Neglect by angels, 113-114
Nephilim, 115-116
Nergal, 114, 153
Newsletters
    Angels Can Fly, 21
    AngelWatch, 26
    Halo Everybody! 15
    Notes & Comments, 26
Newton, Isaac, 114
Nicknames of angels, 115
Nike, 115
Nimrod, 116
    as Orion, 48
Nirvana, 117
Nisroc, 118
Noah, 100, 149

and Raziel Book, 134
and Samael, 32
fed Og, 115
rues writing, 119
Northern Lights
from valkyries, 164
Numbers of angels, 86

**O**
Ode on Intimations of Immortality, 43
Odin, 164
Ofaniel, 65
Og, 115
Origen, 150
angels sealed in grace? 68
on fallen angels, 66
Orion, 48, 149
Out-of-body experience, 111

**P**
Padre Pio, 118-119
Pahaliah, 119
Paine, Thomas, 80
Pandemonium, 95, 106, 110, 169
Paradise, and Ridwan, 137
Paradise Lost, 106, 110, 122, 143
Gabriel's sentries at Eden, 72
Ithuriel, 88
Raphael, Adam, 132
Satan & Uriel, 162
War in Heaven, 167-168
Past lives, 113
Patton, George
talks with God, 36
Pen-Ming, 119

Penemue, 119
Peniel, 53
Persia
Moslems overrun, 11
Dubbiel guards, 60
Pestilence angel, 121
Peter, rescued by angel, 113
Phanuel, 159
Pharaoh, tried in heaven, 165
Philangeli, 121
Phone calls from dead, 64
Physical intervention, 121, 124, 160-61
Poetry and angels, 122
Police, guardian of, 103
Polls, 123-124
and NDE, 112
belief in angels, 38, 124
celestial music, 82
Pope Pius XI
angel conferences, 47
Pope Zachary, 86, 153
Population of angels, 67, 125
Portugal's guardian angel, 66
Postage stamp angels, 126
Powers, 127
Prayers
angel illuminates, 138
Metatron carries, 102
Woven by Sandalphon, 141
Princes, 127
Pseudo-Dionysius, 127, 156
Purgatory, 128
in Judaism, 73
Mary helps souls, 98
seen by Dante, 50
Putti, 128

**Q**
Queen of the Angels, 98

Qui angelorum socius est, 69
Quodlibets, 129
Quotations about angels, 129

**R**
Races of angels, 156
Raguel, 131, 146
    Church attacks, 86
Rahab, 131
    Raziel Book, 134
Rahtiel, 65
Ramiel, 65
Raphael, 132, 153
    and Tobit, 33
    as constellation, 49
    feast day, 15
Rashiel, 65
Rashnu, 133, 170
Raziel, 134 146
Recording angels
    Ben Adhem, 123
    hafaza, 79
    Man in Linen, 96
    Metatron, 102
Regamy, Raymond, 145
Reincarnation, 118
Remiel, 134
Rescues by angels
    Cheri Leslie, 122
    Cokesville School, 45
    Eileen Freeman, 121
    Grace Bulbuka, 112
    Peter, 113
    plane's landing, 63
    William Cowper, 47
Ridwan, 137
Rogo, D. Scott, 64, 81
Rolle, Richard, 81
Rome
    creation of, 72
    watched by Samael, 66

Ronner, John, 13
Ruhiel

**S**
Saints, 138
Samael, 138-139
    and Noah, 32
    beaten by Moses, 16
Sandalphon, 141
Saoshyant, 69
Sariel, 143
Satan, 8, 10, 141
    & Apollyon, 27
    Christ demotes, 36
    description of, 141
    War in Heaven, 167-68
Schiller, Julius, 49
Scientific materialism, 135-36
Sefiroth, 144
Semjaza, 68, 144
Septuagint, 19
Seraphim, 127, 145
Seven archangels, 146
Seven deadly sins, 84, 147
Seven heavens, 146
Sex and angels, 132
    Adam tempted, 139
    apsaras, 28
    huris, 84
Shadrach, Meshach, 17
Shaitans, 147
Shalgiel, 65
Shamshiel, 65, 148
Shemhazai, 148
Sheol, 73, 149
Slavonic Enoch, 18, 158
Smith, Jonathan, 90
Smith, Joseph, 108

Socrates & daimon, 19, 150
Solomon

& magic ring, 133
    Gabriel punishes, 72
Sophia, 150-51
Soubirous, Bernadette, 99
Soul, pre-existence of, 92
Spirit guide, 151
Spiritual warfare
    in Gnosticism, 10
    in heaven, 167-68
    Zoroastrians, 27, 69
Sports & angels, 77
Sraosha, 151, 170
St. Cloud survey, 124
St. Frances of Rome, 138
St. Francisca, 138
St. George, 22
St. Patrick, 165
St. Teresa of Avila, 138
Stamps & angels, 126
Star, as symbol, 30
Steiner, Rudolf, 152
Stevenson, Robert Louis, 130
Stewart, Jimmy, 46
Stigmata of Padre Pio, 119
Still, small voice, 153-54
Stowe, Harriet Beecher, 123
Subconscious mind, 114
Succubi, 58
Suffix angels, 152
Suiel, 65
Summa Theologica, 29, 154
Sun, ruled by Uriel, 162
Sunday, Billy, 80
Superstitions, 156
Swedenborg, Emanuel, 156-7
Swope, Paul, 78
Synchronicity, 46-47

**T**
Take-away apparitions, 55
Talmud, 76

Tamarisk shrub & manna, 97
Taoism & Pen-Ming, 120
Taylor, Terry Lynn, 14, 21
Teachers, guardian of, 161
Telepathy, 16
Testament of Benjamin, 18
Testament of Solomon, 133
Thammuz, 106
Thieves, guardian of, 100
Thought-forms, 157-58
Throne angels, 158
Throne of God, 101, 147
Thrones, 159
Tobias, 132
Torah, 78, 91
Tower of Babel, 15
    built by giants, 115
    ethnarchs, 65
    Nimrod, 116-17
    Mormon dogma, 108
Traffic angels, 77, 159-161
Tree of Knowledge, 62, 91
Tree of Wisdom, 98
Trumpets, as symbols, 30
Tsadkiel, 161
TV angels, 90

**U**
UFOs & Ezekiel, 159
Ur, 31
Uretil, 103
Uriel, 86, 153, 158, 161-2
    feast of, 15
    warns of Flood, 145
Uzza, 164

**V**
Valhalla, 164

Valkyries, 164
Van Ruysbroeck, Jan, 145

Vatican City stamps, 126
Victor, 165
Violent Thrusters, 95
Virgil, 49
Virgin Mary, 71, 98
    constellation, 48
    in World War I, 22-3
    Michael guards, 104
    popularity of, 98
Virtues, 165
Vision quest, 165-6
Visions of children, 44
Vohu Manah, 84, 166
bVoices, 166-67
Voltaire, 80

**W**
War in heaven, 67, 167-8, 172
    and Mammon, 95
    duration of, 168
    in Paradise Lost, 106
    Zoroastrianism, 107
    Michael vs. Satan,
    103
Watkins, Oswald, 23
Weyer, Johann, 114, 168
Wilson, Peter Lamborn, 120
Wine, and Noah, 32
Wings, 116, 169
Wood, C.E.S., 80
Wordsworth, William, 43, 123
World War I & angels, 22
Wormwood, 170
Writers, guardian of, 100
Writing, rued by Noah,119

**X**
Xaphan, 88

**Y**
Yahweh

attacks Israel, 96
Gnosticism, 56, 151
Yazatas, 107, 170
Year of the angels: 1992, 136
Ypres, Battle of, 23

**Z**
Zadkiel, 146, 171
Zafiel, 65
Zagzagel, 171
Zamiel, 65
Zephon, 171
Zipporah, 11
Zohar, 144, 147
Zoroastrian angels
    Mithra, 106
    Rashnu, 133
    Sraosha, 151
    Vohu Manah, 166
    Yazatas, 170
Zoroastrianism, 27
    world ages, 69
    end times, 69
    Holy Immortals, 83-4
    Influenced Jews, 149

# Angel Books and Tapes

The following books and tapes are available at your bookstore or send a check or money order to: **Mamre Press, 107-AK South Second Avenue, Murfreesboro TN 37130**. Please include $1.50 shipping for the first book or tape, 50 cents for each additional book or tape.

**Do You Have a Guardian Angel?** The original best-seller and forerunner of *Know Your Angels*. Seven printings to date. A journalistic and objective look at the subject by a former award-winning newspaper reporter, John Ronner. 192 pages. 49 illustrations. Paperback. $10.95.

**Know Your Angels**. A further exploration of the subject by the same author. Contains much material accumulated by Ronner since the writing of the first book. 192 pages. 17 illustrations. Paperback. $10.95.

**Do You Have a Guardian Angel? (Cassette)**. Here is a 55-minute reading by the author of many of the passages in this well-loved book. Ronner speaks in moving style, narrating some of the touching angel stories, fascinating facts and speculations found in the book. $9.95.

**Know Your Angels (Cassette)**. The author's 55-minute reading of highlights from the book. $9.95.

# The Angel Book Catalog

This newly expanded catalog contains books and sidelines concerning angels. For a free copy, write to: **Mamre Press, 107-AK South Second Avenue, Murfreesboro TN 37130**.

# The Angel Book Catalog

Here is one of the largest sources of angel books anywhere. Looking for a particular angel book? It may well be here, if it is in print. Do you have a new interest in angels? Build an instant library of angel books. Interested in a special variety of angel book, such as fine art or clip art books featuring angels, or a book on how to develop a relationship with a guardian angel, or sidelines like cassettes? This catalog can accommodate you. Although many of the catalog's books are ordinarily hard to find -- you now will have instant access to them, plus the convenience of one-stop shopping.

To receive your FREE copy of this catalog, simply send a stamped (52 cents in postage) self-addressed #10-sized (long) envelope to: Mamre Press, 107-AK South Second Avenue, Murfreesboro TN 37130.